HANG GLIDING:
The Flyingest Flying

HANG GLIDING:

The Flyingest Flying

Text by Don Dedera

Photography by Stephen McCarroll

NORTHLAND PRESS

TITLE PAGE: *Among Pacific squalls Taras Kiceniuk, Jr., soars his Icarus V off the cliffs of Torrey Pines.*

797.55
D
c. 2

Contents

Foreword

I CONSIDER MYSELF VERY FORTUNATE to have been in the right place at the right time to witness and help develop the modern rebirth of hang gliding and ultralight flight. Its many challenges and rewards are especially appealing to me as an ex-model airplane builder, sailplane pilot and engineer, but any one of them is sufficient to attract people from all walks of life. Now almost anyone who ever had the desire to experience the unique sensation of flight can afford to take lessons in hang gliding and possibly own one of these very simple flying machines that weigh so little and are portable enough to carry on small cars.

Here we have what might be termed a total-flight concept available for the special individual who perhaps is able to conceive of his own design, bring it to life in literally just a few weeks, fly it without the need for help from others or special equipment, and know what it is like to explore the ocean of air as only birds and his peers can do. For some, the design challenge is paramount, developing lighter, more efficient structures. Others concentrate on the flying and the rewards it offers, learning all about the micro-meteorology of the earth's boundary layer of air, in slow, quiet flight, the senses exposed directly in the medium; true tactile flight. And there are those who tend to the other aspects of social activity, communication, dispensing news, emphasizing safety, providing the structure of organization that adds cohesiveness to any particular activity.

This book is another step toward wider understanding and appreciation of what hang gliding is all about and it is my pleasure to help introduce it. The many photos will convey an impression that words cannot do justice to, while the words will tell of earlier and recent exploits, and help keep it all in perspective. You should be left with a vivid portrait in your mind, one that, coupled with imagination, might help you see what unexplored possibilities await hang gliding's future.

LLOYD LICHER, *President*
United States Hang Gliding Association, Inc.

The Flyingest Flying

How I yearn to throw myself into
endless space and float above the aweful abyss.

JOHANN WOLFGANG VON GOETHE

1: To Be a Bird

A SPECK SPRINGS AWAY FROM THE CALIFORNIA MOUNTAIN TOP and soars among swatches of scud a thousand feet high. At such distance the figure might be mistaken for a parachute: a translucent canopy and a suspended human figure.

But the man is not the passive dandelion seed he resembles. He flies. Hanging from a few square yards of cloth affixed to a frame of metal tubes, he works his will through three dimensions. By wit and courage and dexterity he turns, dives, circles, climbs and sideslips above ragged ridges and yawning canyons.

Then, when he wishes, he deftly settles onto a landing field no larger than a patio. As the aviator folds his wings a circle of admirers surrounds him to catch his name and ask him questions.

Charles E. Stahl, he says. To friends, Chuck.

When you're not doing this?

I pilot a Boeing 727 for United Air Lines.

For a jet pilot isn't this style of flying rather tame?

Captain Stahl smiles and frowns and smiles again. "Actually, this is the ultimate. When I first aspired to fly I wanted to *be* a bird, not simply fly with the birds, but *be* one. Nothing is nearer to that ideal than being yourself alone with wings in the sky."

Captain Stahl's insight into a new-old sport was uttered at the first annual National Hang Gliding Championships in late 1973 above the San Fernando Valley northwest of

3

Los Angeles. The captain did not win the contest among thirty of the best of the world's hang glider pilots, but he spoke eloquently for the latter-day leaders of a pastime that promises some day to rival the popularity of waterskiing, skin diving, snowskiing, surfing and motorcycling.

"Only in the past several years," says Captain Stahl, "has it become possible for a reasonably handy, coordinated and able-bodied person to go flying safely, using a system that costs only a few hundred dollars, thus far without need of a license. Some of the super pilots are kids with their sharp reflexes and senses, but people of all ages are getting into hang gliding. Look at me." He tugs at a lock of iron gray hair.

Notions of hang gliding are not novel. Humankind's earliest dreams of flight were not of bounding among the craters of the moon in airconditioned suits. Or of flying faster than twice the speed of sound with a hundred thousand pounds of thrust. Or of riding upholstered chairs behind whirring fans.

To be a bird must have appealed to the Neanderthal hunter witnessing an eagle airlift a butchered rabbit to its aerie atop a mountain which he, mere man, must conquer step by laborious step. To this day, humanity holds birdlife in high regard. And why not? Using mysterious navigation and currents, robin-size golden plovers every autumn cross 3,000 miles of open ocean, each bird consuming just two ounces of body fat en route. Within an egg in a nest of floating reeds, a western grebe chick turns and chisels at its thick shell for half

an hour, pops out of its self-made escape hatch, and immediately seeks a cruise on its mother's back. A black-footed albatross needs only to beat its seven-foot wings twice a minute to skim at 30 knots down swells far at sea, hour after hour. Unequaled tourists, Arctic terns migrate 25,-000 miles each year in order to bask in 24-hour daylight at the earth's polar regions.

Such spellbinding specialties were eons in evolving. Consider: since reptiles grew feathers some 150 million years ago, nature has tested and discarded 1,635,000

Mankind's primordial yearnings for flight take wings with birds, which are closely studied by today's hang glider pilots. Grounded by a gale, Jim DeBauche tries to make a bird of a bedspread.

5

plying bird-persons of the 1970s is an A-shaped frame of aluminum tubing fitted with a somewhat larger pie slice of flexible wing, commonly of Dacron sailcloth. The nose angle is 80 to 90 degrees; weight 35 to 40 pounds; 17 to 18 feet along the leading edges; wingspread up to 26 feet. The control bar is a triangle of tubing affixed beneath the frame. Control bar, frame and a top-mounted kingpost are tautly rigged with cables, bolts and turnbuckles. Abaft the control bar dangles the pilot swing seat,

species of birds. Long before man was a factor, birds became extinct at a rate of one species per century. In prehistoric Texas lived and died a gliding reptile half the size of a Boeing 707. The toothed, flightless *Hesperornis* vanished with the warm, shallow seas of mid-America. The tropical parrots of Wisconsin's warm epoch surrendered to the Ice Ages. It was ever thus. Adapt or be doomed. It was the process by which nature chose the 8,600 species of 100 billion birds of this, our world. And it can be argued that this unceasing quest for innovation explains why nature in the middle of the 20th Century brought forth this era's 8,601st species of bird:

    Homo sapiens.

What is new, what makes it plausible, is the wing. From the same space technology that bred the *Saturn V* — 364 feet long with 7.5 million pounds of thrust — came a wing of marvelous and deceptive simplicity, called Rogallo, after its inventor. The Rogallo considered standard by the multi-

or a harness for prone flight. All, it is hoped, is of first rate material meeting the superior standards for aircraft construction. Although it is true that early Rogallos were fashioned of plastic sheeting, elastic nylon together with casually purchased aluminum and even bamboo for framing, and incredibly soft iron wire for rigging, the cost cutting was not without pain. See Chapter VI. Whether at 30,000 feet in a Boeing or 50 feet in a Rogallo, aviation's wry rule applies: "When something goes

6

wrong, there's no place to park up there."
At this writing the price of a sound, well-designed Rogallo of heat-treated tubing, steel aircraft cables and properly stitched Dacron sail is around $600. Helmet and carrying case and a few accessories can add another $100. Nor is hang gliding immune from another of aviation's axioms — a bargain in the hangar can be a loser aloft.

Perhaps no sport ever has grown so greatly, so fast, from scratch. Before 1970 the world held fewer than a hundred hang gliders, nearly all handcrafted by owners. In 1971 the Southern California Hang Glider Association began as the 25-member Peninsula Hang Glider Club under the leadership of Dick Eipper. Within two years membership grew to 5,000, and the name was changed to the United States Hang Gliding Association, Inc. Through 1974 the association added 50 members per month, and at this writing, according to USHGA President Lloyd Licher, new members continue to join at a similar rate.

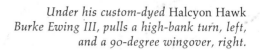

Under his custom-dyed Halcyon Hawk *Burke Ewing III, pulls a high-bank turn, left, and a 90-degree wingover, right.*

Not recommended for beginners, tandem pilots join a soaring scene.

Another Santa Monica-based society, the Self-Soar Association, in 1969 was founded by a dozen hang glider enthusiasts who yearned to exchange data and dreams. Self-Soar now counts 13,000 members, and serves through weekly and quarterly publications as an international forum for hang gliding technology, safety and deeds.

Although one-fifth of the world's hang glider aviators and fans, and the majority of manufacturers, are centered in Southern California, the movement rapidly has spread to Mexico, to Canada, to Europe, to South America, and (did it ever leave?) back Down Under. For American suppliers, dealerships are expanding in Israel, Switzerland, Guatemala, Ecuador, England, Japan, South Africa, New Zealand, Alaska, Hawaii and Guam. Local clubs have sprung

up in virtually all of the United States, and by now the newsletters amount to a paper storm for the Postal Service. Among better known clubs are Ultralite Flyers Organization (UFO) of San Diego, Wings of Rogallo of the San Francisco area, The Northern New Mexico Free Air Force, Pacific Tradewind Sky Sailors of Honolulu, the Foot-Launched Flyers of Michigan, Upward Bound of Montana, and the Outer Limit Society of Tennessee.

In its pell-mell growth, the sport has attracted increasing numbers of critics, who deplore the casualties which have attended all advances in human flight. A sometimes hostile press has tended to report hang glider accidents with the same special sensationalism accorded other aircraft accidents. Among the unimpressed are those who predict hang gliding is merely a fad, and that it will fade away with the hula hoops, roller skates and yo-yos.

RICH TAYLOR: *Down there is Lake Elsinore. Half a mile down there. From where I stand, it's the very definition of flatness. The sun cuts a broad golden streak across it, a hazy glint through the soft wet evening grayness. Between me and the lake are two miles of steeply sloping hillside,*

8

cradling my landing place in an invisible grassy pocket. In a few minutes I'll be there. I hope.

You can only put it off for so long. I take another long look over the edge. A drop of sweat forms on my moustache. I lick it off. My hands start itching in my new gloves, and my Bell Star helmet is fogging up. If I don't go now, I won't be able to see a thing. Besides, the wind is picking up. Pretty soon I'll be dragging my heels backwards across the parking lot when my wing fills. At the base of my throat I can feel that tingling fear like I've just swallowed a mouthful of hot steam. But mostly, I can't stand the suspense.

Forcing an aluminum and Dacron wing that's twenty feet wide into a stiff breeze is work. I heave my body weight into the shoulder harness, and trot heavily toward the cliff edge. Two, three . . . four. The sharp red point of the kite that forms my protective awning dips with my final lunge. I stagger over the cliff, carrying my glider awkwardly.

And suddenly, without warning, I materialize as a graceful swan. I rotate my hips back on the swing seat, stretch my arms forward and attempt to trim the kite. Up comes the nose, centers on the horizon and stays there. Fifty feet off the ground, and like a fledgling sparrow, I'm flying. Me. An uncoordinated humanoid, blessed with only a rudimentary aptitude the dumbest pelican takes for granted. I'm flying.

Leonardo da Vinci would be proud of me. So would Kent Fraunenberger who lived on my block and broke his hand when we were twelve by jumping off the garage roof with a yellow Hi-Flier tied under each arm. Like every other kid who ever dreamed of escaping the mundane by just flying away from it all, I'm serenely gliding over the Southern California landscape, lost in euphoria. A twist of the hips rolls me right. A twitch of the arms, and I yaw left slightly. Pull back, and we dive alarmingly for the earth, sacrificing height for necessary speed. Arms forward, nose up, and we climb into a stall condition.

The stall comes. Even inside a Bell Star, I'm aware of the ever-present wind noise, a cheerful whistle that signifies everything is fine. But in a stall, forward progress stops. And with it, the wind. The wing wants to drop tail first. The giant Dacron sail starts to luff. The flapping drives my arms quickly back, and we jerkily stabilize at a lower, speedier altitude.

Parallel to the slope, I sail down toward the

10

rapidly expanding lake. The wind is back in my ears. Flying becomes a matter of listening for subtle changes. Air pushes against my body from the expected direction and everything is perfect. If it comes from an unexpected quarter, fear crawls up my throat again.

All too soon, my landing spot approaches. . . . The kite dies like a mallard full of shot. I step off onto three feet of air before I find the grass. Not a graceful landing, but I can walk away . . . carrying a dead bird. A short struggle with the harness, and it rests limp on the grass. Helmet off, my body is resting, too. But my mind is already back at the top of the hill, preparing for my next flight. And the next. And the next.

. . . I'm hooked. I admit it.

. . . That's the beauty of hang gliding. Its very simplicity. There's just you. And the wind. The craft itself is the means to the end, and it's unobtrusive enough to be ignored. Your whole consciousness revolves around the sensations, the soaring euphoria of floating over the earth, unfettered, unworried. It's the ultimate escape. But it's more than that, too. It's the fulfillment of one of mankind's oldest desires. To fly, strictly through your own power, with no disruptive engine flailing the air before

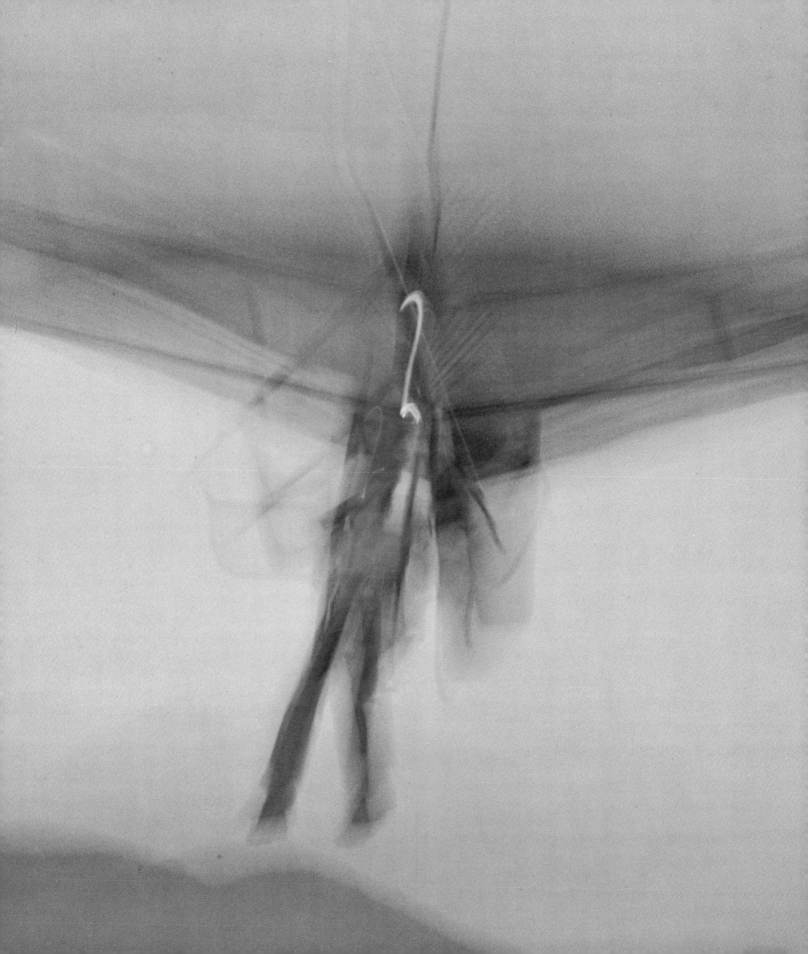

you. To fly, with no protective layer between you and the elements. To fly, really, like a bird. Dependent solely upon your own instincts, your own reflexes, your own skills to sustain effervescent flight.

It's something you can't ever give up . . . natural, innocent, cleansing flight. You, and the kite, the wind and the sun, and the soft gray hills. And far away down the valley floor, Lake Elsinore, beckoning for you to fly to her once more.

In early 1975, at a recreational reserve called Escape Country, the rain-delayed 1974 national championships are winding down with a mixture of speed runs and endurance flights. From 1,500 feet of height the quickest pilots are smoking down the mountain at 30 miles per hour. Other hang gliders which find sun-generated lift along the toast-brown ridges remain in the sky for fifteen minutes and more.

Among the bare-legged young women, friends and pilots, among the elderly spectators with camp chairs and binoculars, among the colorful kites stacked like gigantic colorful butterflies nose down in the wind, among the male aviators who are punctuating their adventure stories with swoops of their palms, strolls a familiar figure. He is Chuck Stahl, tieless but still wearing the airlines uniform for the duty which prevented him from competing in this latest national fly-off.

In the year since he was first met the sport has claimed the life of one of his three sons, all pilots. When Curt Stahl's craft went into a near-vertical dive from which he did not recover, Chuck Stahl was a witness.

The class will come to order. Today's lecturer: Jonathan Livingston Seagull

"It is difficult to bear that loss," says Captain Stahl. "But at age 15 he was in every way a grown man, and I couldn't have kept him from flying. Few men in this world, given a career of many decades, ever become the very best. At his age, among his peers, Curt became as talented a professional hang glider test pilot as existed.

"I console myself in the knowledge that the problem revealed in his last flight will be solved, and that hang gliding will become that much safer. The attainment of human flight has never been without costs."

And with that, Chuck Stahl joins in a discussion of the disconnection mechanism which a hang glider pilot intends to use when he is dropped from a balloon at 20,000 feet of altitude, someday soon.

What a *bird* that will be.

Can any sport be more exciting than flying? Strength and adroitness, courage and decision, can nowhere gain such triumphs as in these gigantic bounds into the air when the gymnast safely steers his soaring machine house-high over the heads of the spectators.

OTTO LILIENTHAL

2: The Pinions of Man

WHAT PRIMORDIAL URGE COMPELLED LILIENTHAL to venture into the realm of the birds? If the Creator had intended for him to fly He would have provided wings and hollow bones and massive breast muscles. In Lilienthal's day the total lack of feathers on human anatomy was generally taken as evidence of God's will. Those who aspired to go aloft not only braved physical dangers, but also the suspicion and ridicule of public opinion, reinforced by divine wisdom.

To dream of flying was heresy. To succeed, a punishable sin.

Thus, under cover of darkness on a summer's night in 1861 the Lilienthal brothers, Gustav and Otto, aged 13 and 14, stole away from their home in the north German province of Mecklenburg. At a military parade ground they donned clumsy wings of beech veneer. Then, imitating storks, the boys for hours ran and flapped, flapped and ran, until they fell exhausted. They did not leave the earth that night, but from this bleak beginning came history's first systematic accumulation of knowledge of aerodynamics.

As a student at a Berlin technical school, as an engineer, as the manager of a machine shop, Otto with Prussian thoroughness scrutinized the builds of various birds. Choosing the gull as his ideal, he tried to translate the secrets of complex flapping into theories for human flight. For years he clung to concepts of moving wings until at last he concluded that a 160-pound man would require pectoral muscles four feet thick to duplicate bird like propulsion.

So Otto returned to basics, to practical inquiries into the performance of rigid, curved

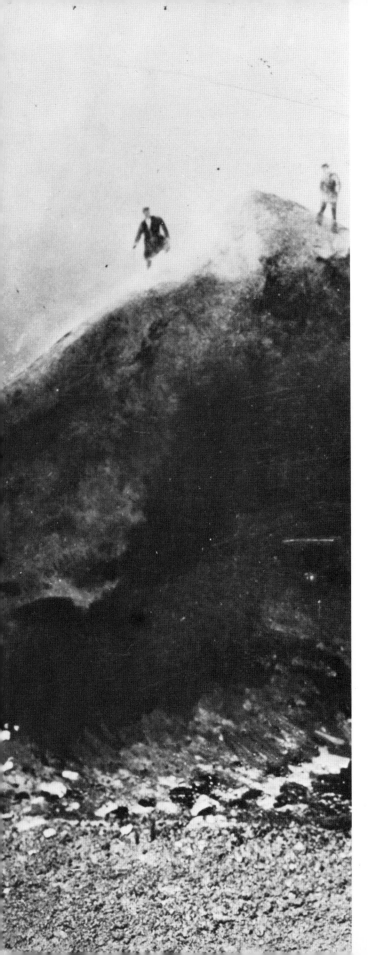

From a man-made hill Otto Lilienthal
flew his batlike gliders near Berlin.

surfaces. Most importantly, he took his experimentation into the air.

"In free flight, in the air," he wrote, "phenomena appear which the experimenter encounters nowhere else . . . and cannot be learned in any other way."

In another of his many papers he described his "sailing apparatus very much like the outspread pinions of a soaring bird. It consists of a wooden frame covered by shirting (waxed cotton muslin). The frame is taken hold of by the hands, the arms resting between cushions, thus supporting the body. The legs remain free for running and jumping. The steering in the air is brought about by changing the center of gravity. This appartus I had constructed with supporting (wing) surfaces of ten to twenty square meters (108 to 215 square feet). The larger sailing surfaces move in an incline of one to eight, so that one is enabled to fly eight times as far as the starting hill is high. . . . The machines weigh, according to their size, from 15 to 25 kilograms (33 to 55 pounds). In order to practice flying with these sailing surfaces one first takes short jumps on a somewhat inclined surface until he has accustomed

21

*Unpowered gliders, such as this
1902 version flown by Wilbur Wright,
predated mankind's giant leap.*

*Octave Chanute appeared at the St. Louis fair with this
hang glider in 1904.*

himself to be borne by the air. Finally he is able to sail over inclines as far as he wishes. The supporting capacity of the air is felt, particularly if there is a breeze. A sudden increase in the wind causes a longer stoppage in the air, or one is raised to a still higher point. The charm of such flight is indescribable, and there could not be a healthier motion or more exciting sport in the open air."

In gaining altitude, he soared, the first man thought to do so. He safely flew 2,000 times in 18 models of gliders (some of which were copied for retail sale to other aeronauts) and Otto's longer flights reached nearly a quarter of a mile. His fame grew as news of his "Bat Flyers" appeared in journals around the world. Overcoming the prejudice of his times, he became the first heroic pilot. He generously shared his findings, as in his major publication, *Bird Flight as the Basis of Aviation.*

Then, one windy August 9, 1896, his luck ran out. In the hills near Rhinow Otto was testing a new method of steering. A gust caught his craft, which stalled, tipped over, and crashed. Next day Otto died, age 49, of a fractured spine.

To his weeping brother, his last words were: "Sacrifices must be made."

Leonardo da Vinci's technical papers on flight contain: "Man when flying must stand free from the waist upwards so as to be able to balance himself as he does in a boat so that the centre of gravity in himself and the machine may counterbalance each other. . . ."

Who, in truth, was the original bird-man? Moderns assume it was one of their kind. It is the sort of tyranny that living civilizations can exercise over those of the ancients. Early man might have flown.

In his world were our own best examples, the birds. Among Cro-Magnon cultures which existed as early as 35,000 years before the present, scientists infer brain power equal to our own. There existed the necessary materials: bamboo, willow wands, and forked limbs for frames; fine skins and thin bark for surfaces; sinew and rawhide for rigging. (In fact, some of the first modern Rogallos were framed with bamboo.)

Cultures proven to be artistic, religious and self-governed might also have possessed the curiosity and skills to mimic flights of birds. That it happened is unknown, but all over the world myths deeply rooted in ancient civilizations speak of human flight. The notion occurs in many old religions, and is mentioned in the Bible. Aztec and Chinese myths predate the most famous flying fantasy of the Greeks, as interpreted by Lorraine Doyle:

Greek mythology tells of Daedalus and his son Icarus, who found themselves imprisoned in a labyrinth on the Isle of Crete. Daedalus fashioned two pairs of large, plumy wings to attach to the shoulders. The fate of crazy Icarus is well known: Once aloft, he began to feel so exhilarated and powerful that he flew higher and higher. The sun melted the wax holding his feathers on, and Icarus found himself cooling his heels in a watery grave. Proving once again that the news media dwell on tragedy, few people know that Daedalus flew all the way to Sicily, where he landed, built a temple, and hung up his wings.

During historic times, as with so many things, Leonardo da Vinci, the genius of the Renaissance, blazed the scientific trail to human flight. By studying birds and

24

falling leaves, he learned about airflow and drag. He invented a parachute of linen, which a man could use to descend "from any great height without sustaining injury." The master's sketches of flying machines included a model which the pilot was to fly prone, flapping his wings with leg power and activating his elevator by means of a harness attached to his head. The concepts were somewhat flawed, and as is recorded, they never flew. Neither did a series of contraptions concocted by the "tower jumpers" of the Middle Ages. Entrusting life and limb to handcrafted wings, a dreary succession of brave but puny humans demonstrated time and again that the most furious beating of arms could not generate lift relative to that achieved by birds.

Then, after centuries of such bone-smashing research, the yearning to fly found another mode: lighter-than-air. Hung up on hot air and hydrogen, humanity in astonishing numbers ventured into the wild blue yonder beneath bulbous balloons. In the late 1700s the search for pure, avian flight was all but abandoned.

26

During national championships, a closed-cockpit sailplane soars across Black's Beach, California.

Off a mountain near Los Angeles leaps a prototype rigid-wing hang glider.

One who remained at the drawing board was Sir George Cayley, a Yorkshire baronet of vast ingenuity. As others before him, Cayley began with meticulous observations of feathered friends. He realized that wings must produce lift not only for weight, but also to overcome drag. He built numerous model wings and tested them in moving air. Years of research culminated in 1804 in his first model glider. Exactly when Cayley constructed his full-sized craft is questionable; his activities were hushed up by his embarrassed family. By some accounts Cayley himself in 1809 flew a hang glider, which some historians accept as the first airplane. Better documented are Cayley's gliders of 1849, piloted by a small boy on a short hop, and of 1853. The latter craft gained airspeed by rolling on wheels down a hill, to glide some 1,500 feet across a shallow valley, only to crack up against the other side. The reluctant aviator was Cayley's coachman, who miraculously emerged from the wreckage unscathed, but permanently disenchanted. He is said to have shouted, "I was hired to *drive*, not to *fly!*"

27

Early on, the diehard devotees of heavier-than-air flight thought to power their craft with engines. One William S. Henson's steam propulsion was defeated by weight, in a scale model tested in 1848. Others experimented with rubber bands and compressed air, resulting in "flights" as artfully sustained as that of a toy balloon turned loose with its mouthpiece open. Life was precarious but adventurous souls spread the word to new lands.

Interest in aviation crossed the Atlantic only to be met by bitter provincial prejudice. In the *First Century of Flight in America*, Jeremiah Milbank, Jr., writes:

The early pioneers of modern aviation were at first looked upon as lunatics or at best foolhardy visionaries. . . . It was for this reason that in the 1880's and 1890's many flying-machine experiments were conducted secretly under the cover of darkness or in such remote locations as to discourage even the most curious of spectators.
Such were the circumstances under which it is supposed that the first successful flight in a glider was accomplished in this country by John Joseph Montgomery, a 26-year-old Californian. The year was 1883.

On August 28 before dawn Montgomery and his brother, James, freighted by wagon a glider of their own manufacture to a dusty hill near the Mexican border south of San Diego, California. Their craft had two wings, each ten feet long and averaging four and one-half feet in width. A horizontal tail could be elevated or depressed through a system of cords and pulleys. Suspended beneath the frame was a bicycle seat for the pilot.

Daylight brought a sea breeze across Otay Mesa, and when a gust lifted one of the exaggerated airfoils, John announced he was ready. James grabbed a long tow rope and ran down the hill against the wind. Suddenly he felt the rope slacken. He looked up and directly above him John was soaring with 50 feet of altitude. With James chasing, John glided an estimated 600 feet. John flew many times that day.

The weakness of this story is that by the time it was told years later not a scrap of

the glider remained. There were no photographs, and no witnesses, other than James. Those who accept the statements of the brothers Montgomery consider John's achievement to be the first controlled flight of a heavier-than-air craft in America.

That John Montgomery was an inventive aviator and accomplished tinkerer is beyond doubt. His flights in self-designed hang gliders after 1904 are well documented and give some insight into how the first craft may have been made. In 1911 Montgomery was killed in the crash of one of his machines.

Whether he was first to fly, even before Lilienthal, may never be settled to everyone's satisfaction. But whether he *could* have flown currently is being answered. Through the International Aerospace Hall of Fame a $1,500 prize is offered to the first contemporary birdman who can recreate Montgomery's alleged flight of 1883. Detailed rules and specifications insure that the materials and designs of Montgomery will be used, insofar as safety and technology permit.

Pilcher, Ader, Wenham, Bleriot, Moui-

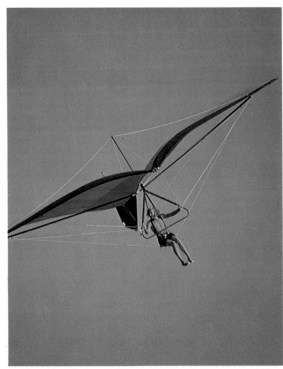

In a gentle S-turn, Jack Schroder tests an early version of the Seagull V.

llard, Hargrave, Pénaud — the list of contributors to hang gliding is not long. Following Lilienthal, Octave Chanute kept the faith. As an engineer of such stature that he bridged the Mississippi, Chanute was familiar with the Pratt truss, a method of bracing rectangular members with diagonal stiffeners. Chanute applied the Pratt principle to a biplane glider whose wings were stiffened by struts and wires. While in his 60s Chanute took up hang gliding from the sand hills of Lake Michigan, near Chicago. During the final years of the last century Chanute and his employees logged thousands of flights without accident. It's told that Chanute mastered full stall landings through observations of a sparrow touching down on pavement.

But Chanute's niche in aviation history is most secure in his drive to assist and support other inventors, wherever they were in the world. For 35 years until his death in 1910 he strove for free exchange of data among independent thinkers in aviation. As noted by the *FAA Aviation News*, "Chanute's inability to take the final step in the perfection of the glider, as per-

ceived by the Wrights (controlled, movable planes), cost him any claim to immortality as an inventor; but it may very well be that his willingness to formulate the problem for the benefit of others made it possible for Wilbur and Orville to grasp the solution." The Wright brothers and Chanute exchanged 400 letters.

Somehow lost in the rush and thunder of the seven decades since Kitty Hawk is general appreciation of the Wright brothers as glider builders and pilots. Considerable study preceded construction of their full-sized tailless biplane of 1900. A horizontal control surface was placed forward of the wings, which could be warped for lateral control. Although this new control method

*Certain to draw a crowd, a new model introduces a
rudder to Rogallo flight.*

worked, the Wrights were disappointed with the overall performance of this glider and their second, a larger biplane flown in the summer of 1901. Questioning the validity of the findings of their predecessors, the Wrights built a wind tunnel for testing wing shapes. By 1902 the Wrights knew more about curved flying surfaces "a hundred times over" than any inventors of the past. Of their laboratory work, they wrote, "We saw that the calculations upon which all flying machines had been based were unreliable, and that all were simply groping in the dark. Having set out with absolute faith in the existing scientific data, we were driven to doubt one thing after another, we cast all aside. . . . Truth and error were everywhere so intimately mixed as to be indistinguishable."

The new wing that emerged from the Dayton, Ohio, wind tunnel achieved stability through the use of less camber (curve) in the wing, and ratio of greater wing length to width. The third Wright glider biplane, with a wing span of 32 feet, car-

ried the brothers on nearly a thousand flights in autumn, 1902, near Kitty Hawk, North Carolina. Their emphasis on safety serves as a model of maturity in attitude toward the ideals of flight.

Next year the Wrights were back at Kitty Hawk with the *Flyer*, a machine which would virtually halt hang gliding for half a century. Midships in the *Flyer* sputtered a 13-horsepower engine which by straining for 12 seconds induced flight, "the first in the history of the world in which a machine carrying a man had raised itself by its own power into the air in full flight, had sailed forward without reduction of speed, and had finally landed at a point as high as that from which it had started."

Thereafter, in geometric leaps, humanity would advance the state of the art to *Jenny* to *Trimotor* to *Gooney Bird* to *Spitfire* to *Starfighter* to 707 to *Sputnik* to SST to *Apollo 11*.

And for a while, at least, the flyingest flying would be forgotten.

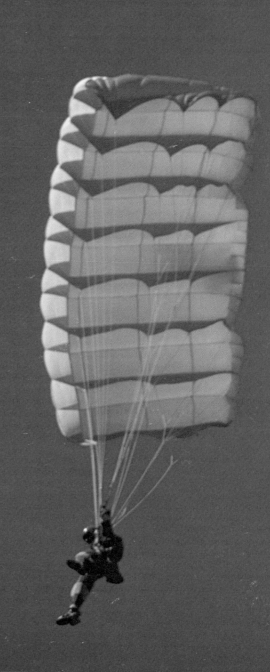

In developing aviation, in making it a form of commerce, in replacing the wild freedom of danger with the civilized bonds of safety, must we give up this miracle of the air? Will men fly through the sky without seeing what I have seen, without feeling what I have felt? Is that true of all things we call human progress — do the gods retire as commerce and science advance?

CHARLES A. LINDBERGH

3: On Gossamer Wings

VERY MUCH ALIVE AT THIS WRITING IS JACK IRWIN, whose 82 years more than span humanity's incredible step from Carolina sand to Moon dust. Spry and bright, he grants interviews to writers at his home in Bolinas, near San Francisco. When aviation was accelerating away on its power binge to faster, higher, heavier — and abstracted — flight, Irwin tried to hang in, as a hang glider pilot.

At 13, his hunger to fly was so intense, he volunteered to substitute for a carnival parachute jumper who one Sunday failed to show up for work.

"Like a damn fool I said sure, I'd jump. I weighed maybe 100 pounds. The 'chute was made for a man who weighed 150 pounds more than that. I went up to 400 or 500 feet and probably jumped too soon. Anyway, oh, was it nice! I floated down like a butterfly. I was paid a $20 gold piece, the most money I'd ever seen. But when my folks found out, they put a stop to it."

Very well, there was more than one way to pluck a bird. When 15 years old, without benefit of a kit, or plan, or expert advice, he built his own hang glider of split spruce and rubberized diaper fabric.

"You had a couple of parallel rods, no straps," he recalls. "You'd hang on by your armpits and run and jump. If you could last eight seconds, you were flying. Want to go up, you'd hold your feet out ahead. Most flights were 30 to 45 seconds. A few times we'd last a couple of minutes."

Irwin's may have been the original factory for hang gliders. He built and sold them in

35

Multiplying the forces of gravity in a 360-degree turn, a Rogallo pilot toys with a thousand feet of altitude.

Auburn, in the Sierra Nevada foothills. But demand steadily declined, and he, too, was swept up in the roar and fumes. During the 1920s he built about a hundred Meteorplanes, little 20-horsepower biplanes of spruce and muslin (one of which is permanently displayed in the Oakland Museum). Irwin shipped plans and parts for hundreds more Meteorplanes to all parts of the world. The airplane weighed 240 pounds and cost $1,165 ready-to-fly, or $365 in a kit.

"You could buy parts for the fin for $3.50, and you were building an airplane," Irwin remembers. "And the next order would come in for the tailpiece for $12.50. Maybe the fellow would get into trouble with his mother, and she would burn it up, or maybe he wouldn't finish it."

Lindbergh's trans-Atlantic flight of 1927 so stimulated sales, "We were selling airplanes faster than we could make them. There were so many people calling I had the telephone taken out. That year I made 50,000 bucks.

". . . But Congress wanted to make aviation safe. They began regulating. The smaller outfits couldn't stand the expense. A lot of us went under."

The race for performance, comfort and safety at all costs grew tremendously expensive. In lockstep with technical ad-

36

vances arrived governmental regulations, *ad infinitum,* until the ownership and maintenance of a private airplane became in effect the privilege of the rich. Aviation retained its romantic aura around Richtofen, Doolittle, Earhart, Post and the like, but as cockpits evolved into airborne offices and passenger compartments into cocktail lounges, much of the glory of simple birdlike flight was lost.

And when the time came for a gigantic pioneer himself to advise his son regarding a career in aviation, Jon Lindbergh says:

My father recommended against it. He felt that aviation had progressed from the pioneering phase into a highly skilled but nevertheless routine profession. Pilots were now enclosed in cockpits and surrounded by sophisticated instruments, rather than the open air, and "flying by feel" which he so much loved. Routine commercial aviation was, of course, the goal of much of his life's work. But with that accomplished, he felt that if he were starting out, say, in 1950, instead of 1925, probably he would choose another career.

Meantime, claiming to keep the faith in self-flight were enthusiasts of other sports: balloonists, sky divers, man-powered flyers, sailplane pilots. But those who as-

cended in bags of gas experienced silence and height at the expense of maneuverability and convenience. Free-falling spirits who for fleeting moments performed hurtling acrobatics were obliged to get high as prisoners of power and return to earth as parachutists. Sailplane soaring, too, departed from the lyric of Lilienthal to express another form of poetry for enclosed pilots reading panels of gauges and deploying airfoils refined by computers. When a rebel (such as Volmer Jensen on the West Coast in the 1940s) revived a rigid-wing hang glider capable of soaring, he was patronized as a likeable, but peculiar, old coot.

At long last, even those stubborn believers in the age-old scheme of man-*powered* flight finally achieved it — for short hops in ultralight contrivances which wrung the last foot-pound of energy from the human leg. Still, avian flying for the masses remained as remote as the myth of Icarus.

Two men accorded major credit for conjuring up an elemental, universal means of human flight are Francis M. Rogallo and William Bennett. Thoroughly different in intent and technique, they were in their work a half a world apart.

Rogallo, the meticulous scientist, is a native Californian in retirement at Kitty Hawk, North Carolina. Soon after earning

a graduate degree in mechanical engineering at Stanford University he joined the Langley Research Center at Hampton, Virginia, in 1936. Largely his work was with wind tunnel testing and stability and control questions of conventional aircraft. When the center became part of the National Aeronautics and Space Administration, Rogallo supervised research in Langley's full-scale testing division.

On the job, he abetted aviation's noisy progress through the sonic barrier into the fringes of interplanetary space. But in his spare time, he dabbled in designs for portable, flexible, controllable sails. At first he had no practical purpose — the "aerophilosophical problem: could you design a

38

Like a moth from an outsize cocoon, Ken Wagner's *Bennett Delta Wing emerges from its sailcloth case.*

In kite loading lane, pilots in competition wait for a truck to carry them to the top of a hill.

39

wing that somehow was held in shape by the action of the air itself."

Or in Rogallo's own words: "A parachutelike tension structure in which the wing surface shape is maintained by the balance of forces between the airload on the surfaces and the tension in the suspension lines, and flexible wings that could have several types of localized stiffening."

Experimentation with models of sail area as large as 30 square feet led to an application in 1948 for a patent for a flexible, delta-wing kite in the names of Rogallo and his co-inventor and wife, Gertrude. For nearly a decade Rogallo cast about for practical uses and financial backers. The government foresaw no need for the Rogallo wing. For two years a toy firm (the makers of Silly Putty) manufactured a child's kite which was a superb flyer, but at $3 a copy, priced out of sight. The Rogallos realized no more than a few hundred dollars from that enterprise. Since their comprehensive patent expired in 1968, before the sport of hang gliding zoomed, the wonder wing has brought the Rogallos little more than fame.

40

*Killing his airspeed in a controlled stall, a pilot
approaches the landing zone in national competition.*

The same *Sputnik I* that touched off the space race drew attention to far out equipment, including the Rogallo wing. It seemed to offer one means of bringing rocket hardware back to earth intact. In 1963 the Rogallos gave the government rights to their patents, some 25 in all, for a royalty fee. At Langley, Rogallo elaborated upon his ideas. Elsewhere, his thoughts were tested by every flying character except Mary Poppins, Dumbo and Santa Claus.

Rogallo wings were made into gliders, some of which soared. Some were towed; some were powered. Others were dropped. Still others were deployed from launch vehicles as high as 200,000 feet. For the Army, Jeeps obligingly leaped aloft under Rogallo wings. A canopy called the Parasev was fabricated by NASA and was safely demonstrated through 5,000 feet of descent by Test Pilot Milt Thompson. Astronauts Gus Grissom and Neil Armstrong also flew the Parasev.

Yet they are not considered to be the first true Rogallo pilots. In 1961 Barry Hill Palmer, a Northern Californian on the mailing list for NASA reports, handcrafted a Rogallo wing, and by running and jumping, made brief flights from sand dunes. Palmer generally is accepted as Number One to achieve foot-launched human Rogallo flight. At about the same time a North Carolina engineer, Thomas Purcell, Jr., went aloft in his home-built Rogallo under tow at the Raleigh-Durham Airport. Purcell is credited with first flying a towed Rogallo.

After them, any crediting of individuals for innovations will win you more arguments than a politically inspired beauty contest with religious overtones. It is probably important that Richard Miller built himself a plastic covered Rogallo nicknamed the "Bamboo Butterfly" with $9 worth of materials, and in 1964, flew it. Next year another engineer, Jim Natland, paid Kenny Watts, famous West Coast

42

sailmaker, to fit a frame with Dacron. He astonished bathers and golfers by sailing off of dunes at Palos Verdes, California, and the 10th tee of a golf course in Huntsville, Alabama. Irv Culver's expertise over the years has guided countless improvements. In his book, *Hang Gliding, the Basic Handbook of Skysurfing*, Dan Poynter names Dave Kilbourne as first to soar a Rogallo, in 1971. These, and two dozen more, deserve mention as pacesetters.

That said, if one chap ranks alongside Francis Rogallo, he is Bennett, the self-styled Australian Birdman. Long before American civilians were into Rogallos, Bennett was nearly killing himself flying kites Down Under. Bennett and a fellow Aussie, Bill Moyes, fluttered aloft on flat, grossly unstable sails by towing them behind motorboats and shussing them down ski slopes, as early as 1956.

"Flat kites are an invention of the devil," says Bennett. "If we ever did anything right in those days, it was because we did everything wrong beforehand. If our test flights had been over solid ground, we'd have died a thousand times. Instead, we crashed into water and snow. In the process we learned something about control."

Meanwhile, NASA papers reached John Dickinson, an electronics engineer of Gosford, New South Wales. He induced Bennett and Moyes to construct tow kites of Rogallo configuration. Scarred and bruised, they eventually flew Rogallo shapes higher than anybody had taken flat kites. Once a tow boat hit a sandbar, leaving Bennett no alternative than to glide down to a surprisingly adroit landing, which led to their cutting loose on purpose thereafter.

The control apparatus devised by Bennett-Moyes is beautifully simple: a rigidly mounted trapeze bar of tubing, and a child's swing seat. Whereas Palmer and Natland had hung beneath their Rogallos on parallel bars *a la* Lilienthal, the delta wings of the Aussies afforded pinpoint control. On April 29, 1969, Bennett arrived to begin his conquest of the United States in a hang glider.

As one writer put it, "It can be truly said that never before in so short a time has one man exposed a new sport to so many unbelieving eyeballs and so many feet of home-movie film."

He soared over the Golden Gate to land on Alcatraz. A James Bond movie was inspired by his stunts. On Independence Day, Bennett spiraled down the Statue of Liberty to earn a stern reprimand from the New York harbor police. Bennett was hired to thrill tourists at Lake Tahoe, Wisconsin Dells and Cypress Gardens. For a television ad he hung in there for 34 miles behind a

44

car from one cove on Lake Mead to another. He dropped from a mile-high mountain to below sea level at Death Valley. Towed behind a speedboat on Arizona's Lake Havasu, he set an altitude record of 2,960 feet. Meanwhile, Bennett's chum Moyes piloted a hang glider from the rim to the bottom of Grand Canyon (and was fined $150 "for holding a special event in a national park without a permit").

Between sensations Bennett preached that hang gliders were reliable, inexpensive, portable, inherently safe and fun to fly, once the sport was mastered. Not unexpectedly, his airborne evangelism won the earliest congregation of converts in that crucible of American lifestyles, Southern California. Suddenly the skies over the beach dunes of Playa del Rey beyond the runways of Los Angeles International Airport were filled with hang gliding fledglings honing their skills against Pacific breezes. The boom was on.

Ironically, as the new sport involved thousands in its sweep from the West Coast to the East, it eventually ensnared the man who made it possible. In February, 1974, at age 62, Francis Rogallo took up hang gliding as a way to keep in good physical shape. The walking back uphill, he says, aids circulation. At latest count, Rogallo had logged his hundredth flight from his Carolina sand dune.

In recognition of Rogallo's "unique and outstanding contribution to foot-launched, fuel-less, ultralight flight in the United States" he was awarded the highest non-competitive honor of the U.S. Hang Gliding Association, the Ed Gardia Memorial Trophy. At the awards ceremony, a thunderous, standing ovation followed the final words of association president Lloyd Licher:

"Thank you, for giving us wings to fly."

As a pilot sprints down a rocky slope, air grabs sailcloth, and a Pacific Gull kite takes to the sky.

*It is plain that life on earth has suddenly quickened. One
generation has leapt off a horse's back and through the sonic wall.
Life moves naturally upward in a spiral, but here the spiral is
bent strangely, before continuing its accelerating, buoyant course.
It is the way of things important to life. It is irregular, not entirely
predictable, but continuing: the motion of air under wings that hold
up airplanes and birds, the flow of blood, the breath of consciousness,
the growth of stars, even the prophetic revelations of God.*

GUY MURCHIE

4: Fabulous Flings

THE DAY IS OCTOBER 26, 1973, the first since September forecast for winds of less than
30 miles per hour. A struggling helicopter crabs along the craggy massif which forms the
French-Italian frontier. At 15,766 feet above sea level, at the very summit of Mont Blanc,
the tallest peak in Europe, the whirlybird gently touches down. Men step out, and crouch-
ing beneath the hissing rotors, unload an elongated sack of tubing, cloth and cables. While
the helicopter spins off to fetch a camera crew, Rudy Kishazy, a 30-year-old electrician
from Plymouth, Michigan supervises the assembly of his Bill Bennett kite. Kishazy's face
and ears are smeared with grease to protect against the 15-degree temperature. He gasps in
the thin air.

*Finally . . . everything is ready. The view is magnificent, just mountain peaks all around,
and 13,000 feet below, the valley disappearing in and out of the clouds and fog. It looks
strange, and I keep saying to Jerry, I've got to make it, I've got to make it. Jerry answers,*
Sure you will.
*I begin to get tired and sluggish and a little headachy. . . . It is 4 p.m. when I get the signal.
I squeeze the bar. I'm not afraid, but I feel like fighting. I am getting very mad and I feel I
just have to win. As I take off, I can't see too well. I ski down the northeast side which is
forty-five, fifty degrees of ice wall. I am just speeding and speeding. I hear a sharp noise
when the sail is grabbed by the wind, warning me that I have the right takeoff speed. I
push the handle bar out but no response. My thoughts begin getting mixed up. There is not*

49

tow-launched kite is poised for a series of 360-degree turns around the observation tower at Sea World marine park in San Diego.

From a site in Pio Pico Park where
John J. Montgomery is thought to have flown,
modern hang gliders gather.

enough air for the takeoff, *I think. Suddenly, a funny feeling jerks me awake, as if a fast elevator has stopped. The wind is blowing in my face and I am shouting, I made it, I made it!*

The view is breathtaking and I am just speeding, fighting with the turbulences. Catching a strong updraft, I just glide. I lose the mountain. I just shoot out into space. It looks as if the whole world stops, and I feel as if I don't belong to it anymore. The clouds are dense, and getting in my way. But slowly I can see through the clouds and fog into the valley. . . . I start looking for my landing spot. It rapidly

comes up towards me, and I level off and land. I am down, hanging on to the bar, trying to dream a little bit longer. I am not sure everything has come true. But in no time, the crowd gathers around me and I am fully awake. I am tired, but I feel wonderful. My dream has come true. And I feel richer — with a memory that only a few people share with me.

Kishazy's descent from the top of Europe to the valley of Servoz consumed 13,142 feet of altitude, 30 minutes of time and more than 15 miles of distance, under a Rogallo-type wing that just a few years earlier was considered merely a plaything of the soft, sandy beach. Nor was the flight a fluke. It was the culmination of a long summer of flings off two-mile high Grands Montets and Petite Aiguille Verte into mobs of adoring French citizens and admiring newspersons, who dubbed him, *L'homme Volant.*

In its brief half-a-decade, the world's freshest species of bird surprised even that old, poetic aviator, Murchie, who as the navigator of a trans-Atlantic cargo airplane in 1954 also wrote, "There may come a day when men, through long controlled genetics, have adapted their bodies in size and shape to gliding or flying. I don't see much sign of it yet as I glance at

Getting it together, a hot air balloon lifts a hang glider to 3,000 feet for a drop over Trabuco Canyon, California.

my fellow crew members at work around me, sitting, writing figures into forms like so many bookkeepers."

Bookkeeper, indeed. Kishazy repeated his Mont Blanc stunt, and at latest reports, was heading for the highest peak in Africa, 19,565-foot Kilimanjaro.

By now, launches from lesser mountains, a mile or so in elevation, are routine. Dick Eipper celebrated his 27th birthday by running off 10,023-foot Haleakala Volcano in his *Flexi-Flyer* and traveling more than nine miles to a landing 1,500 feet above sea level. Gordy Cummings flew 14,110-foot Pikes Peak, and Dave Gibas topped him by tripping off 14,264-foot Mt. Evans, also in Colorado.

A flight of 50 miles was attained in New Zealand. In mid-1974 Mt. Fuji, at 12,388 feet Japan's highest mountain, was claimed by Mike Harker of Newport Beach, California, who flew 12.5 miles and 23 minutes until forced down by fog. A year earlier the same Harker may have become the first person to fly legally from one country to another by hang glider, when he skiied off the 10,000-foot crest of Germany's Zugspitz into an Austrian valley. He gained permission of authorities by filing a flight plan and paying a fee of 30 marks. *Kurz nach dem Start wäre Harker beinahe von einer Bö an den Felsen geschmettert wor-*

den. Dann aber schwebte er ruhig wei ein Condor auf die österreichische Seite nach Ehrwald hinunter. (Shortly after takeoff a gust nearly threw Harker against the mountain. But then he glided as calm as a condor down to Ehrwald on the Austrian side of the mountain.)

Perhaps the oddest alliance of the world's new bird has been with those throwbacks to another era, the free-flying, hot-air balloonists. Bill Moyes, in 1972, is thought to be the first to launch a hang glider from a balloon, in Australia. Bob Kennedy and Bill Bennett dropped from a balloon at California's Lake Elsinore in 1970. Later flights were made by Dave Kilbourne and Donnita Holland at Lake Suc-

At the first annual World Hang Gliding Championship a pilot seeks a target during qualifications. The winner was Greg Mitchell.

Nose down into mild wind, kites await fresher breezes for launches at Torrey Pines.

cess also in California. For a while Kilbourne of San Francisco held the record of releasing at 9,600 feet of altitude. Then, in late 1974, Dennis Kolberg, 22, of Walnut Creek, California, doubled his pleasure by riding his Rogallo down from 17,000 feet above Morgan Hill, some 70 miles south of San Francisco. The flight lasted 35 minutes. Sharing in the record-breaking was balloonist Brent Stockwell, 43, of Union City, California. But with ascensions in the works all over, no one can foretell where the race to altitude will end.

This isn't to say higher is better. Gary Chaudior, a ski instructor at Aspen, Colorado, got it all together in mid-1974 with balloonist Ben Abruzzo of Albuquerque, New Mexico. From a release at 3,000 feet, Chaudior landed exactly upon his point of ascension. At about the same time Ted Farrell lifted Dave Muehl and his hang glider to 2,500 feet over California City Airport, about 80 miles north of Los Angeles. Although Muehl had launched by

foot from greater heights, he was impressed by "the purity of the experience — no mountains to climb — just flying, one kind on the way up, another on the way down. It was one of my most colorful, aesthetic flights." In May of 1974 Dan Chapman of Marlboro, New York, may have been first with a balloon drop *at night*. With authorities properly notified Chapman was plucked by a balloonist to 1,500 feet above Kobelt Airport, Wallkill, New York.

The air was dead calm and the lift-off and short ride to altitude were uneventful. The release system did not work, so we used our back-up system. He cut me loose with a knife. The release was perfect (we were descending at cut-away), no problem. Runway lights were on and I flew down the runway to a stand-up landing in front of about 30 witnesses, astonished pilots, etc.!

Claims for another kind of hang gliding superlative are beclouded by imprecise measurement. Who has, after launch by foot or balloon, *gained* the most altitude? In 1973 Ronnie Rondel in a Delta flyer stepped off 1,600-foot Dyna Soar Mountain near Acton, California and immediately caught a thermal which added an estimated 1,500 feet to his distance above the earth, as confirmed by witnesses. But with glide ratios of fixed-wing hang gliders rivaling sailplanes, and refined Rogallos joining the soaring skies, the gaining of altitude from launch height is becoming commonplace. San Diego's Burke Ewing recently at Elsinore rode a thermal upward for what he guessed was 2,000 feet, which may be a record. Until pilots of hang glid-

ers can support their claims with competent instruments, this category will attract much controversy.

Endurance is something else. The clocks of this time-conscious civilization can be quite accurate. Just who deserves honors for some of the earlier, extended flights is questionable, but hang glider historian Carol Boenish Price recognizes Dave Kilbourne's accomplishment at Mission Ridge, near San Jose, California, as the first noteworthy endurance flight of a Rogallo wing. Kilbourne kept it up 1 hour 4 minutes, on September 6, 1971.

On July 2, 1972, Taras Kiceniuk, Jr. foot-launched his *Icarus II* fixed-wing, 32-foot span, tailless glider from the 340-foot coastal cliff north of San Diego. First to dare to fly such cliffs, on that day Kiceniuk prolonged his high 1 hour 11 minutes. Kiceniuk with an airspeed indicator measured

New colors, new configurations continue to enliven hang glider art and design.

*The ultimate high for some pilots
in cliff soaring is to reach uppermost position
on a day of ideal soaring conditions.*

flying speeds of 22 miles per hour with the landing gear down (that is, sitting upright) and 25 miles per hour with the gear up (in supine position).

Rising to the challenge next was Bob Wills of Santa Ana, California. A solid 200-pounder, Wills induced Bill Bennett to construct a special large Rogallo, which on September 7, 1972, at Palmdale north of Los Angeles, kept Wills aloft for 2 hours 16 minutes.

The combination of Kiceniuk, Torrey Pines, and *Icarus II* could not be denied. October 29, 1972: 2 hours 26 minutes.

This brought an invasion from Wills himself at Torrey Pines, on December 7, 1972. First to fly a Rogallo off Torrey,

Wills that day extended the record to 3 hours 3 minutes.

Something of a Wrong-Way Corrigan of hang gliding was Tony Kolerich, in his endurance flight of April 13, 1973. Under his home-modified, black plastic *Flexi-Flyer*, he took off at Torrance Beach, California, at 4:21 p.m. in soaring conditions just for the hell of it. Numbed and bruised by his harness, Kolerich crash-landed without injury on the beach after dark with a new endurance record: 3 hours 9 minutes.

The mark stood three months. Riding the zephyrs of an advancing storm at Torrance, Pat Conniry extended the record to 3 hours 36 minutes, on July 15, 1973.

Featherlight Mike Mitchell next claimed the honor for the longest flight. In a *Seagull III*, in winds so faint that others dared not to fly, teen-age Mitchell was able to soar at Torrey Pines for 3 hours 45 minutes.

There followed four assaults whose effect was to demonstrate that enduring hang gliding flight was as much or more a test of human blood circulation, mental concentration, nutrition and waste systems, as pilot skill and aircraft performance. On September 1, 1973, Bob Wills rode the trade winds at Waimanalo Bay, Oahu, Hawaii, for 5 hours 6 minutes. The sensational event was shown on live tele-

Maintaining lift in a thermal, Bill Liscomb uses a rudder and weight shifting to control his Quicksilver fixed-wing glider.

vision. Two days later Pat Conniry took advantage of ideal conditions at the near-vertical face of Buff's Cove, Palos Verdes, California. Result: 5 hours 21 minutes. Wills was back in the lift at Waimanalo September 15. So constant and vigorous are the winds of the northeast face of the Koolau Range, local records attest that persons have jumped or fallen 200 feet down sheer cliffs and survived, their descent slowed by uplift. Once, a man attempting suicide was huffed and puffed back up to where he had leaped. In such flow, Wills regained the glory: 8 hours 24 minutes. The achievement vaulted Wills into national fame. Not until March 17, 1974, did a rival pilot, John Hughes, leap at Waimanalo and not alight for 10 hours 5 minutes.

As Chris Price comments, "Flying for 10 or more hours now has about the same significance as pole sitting. Such marathon flights only prove that the wind blows for a long time in certain places."

60

Much can be said, also, for hang gliding as a spectator sport. As Rogallos in butterfly decor wheel and whisper at Waimanalo, candlelit diners watch from cliffside patios. Along the flyingest beaches of California, throngs of rubbernecks turn their faces skyward. At Torrey enthusiastic nonfliers clamber far out on the headland, to shout approval to the soaring pilots, and peer at the nudeniks sprawled under the sun on Black's Beach. At Tennessee's Mount Aetna tourists and residents from nearby Chattanooga take the tram to a park where they watch hang gliders launch into an airway three-fourths of a mile long across a thousand feet of descent. One does not have to be a pilot to enjoy hang gliding. The spectacle is quiet, pollution-free and generally without charge for admission. Vicariously, humans grounded by physical shortcomings and lack of nerve may also act out the Icarian dream of strapping on a pair of wings and flying.

*Unique, spread-eagle style of Bob Wills serves to
convert his body into an air brake to slow for landing.*

*In marginal winds for Rogallo gliders, a sailplane
finds sufficient lift to maintain altitude in cliff soaring.*

By now, the artistry of pilots and craft is such that Rogallo wings are maneuvered into whip stalls, chandelles, spiral dives, 360-degree turns, steep dives, lazy-eight turns and hammerhead stalls. (Only by experts, it is hoped.) Can loops be far away? "By loop we don't mean the sloppy of sloppies: standing it on the tail and falling backwards," says Tom McMillan. "We mean pulling positive gravity all the way around. The obvious question is, 'How dirty can it be, and still keep airspeed over the top?' " And the obvious next question is, "If loops are included in repertoires of hang gliders, if the pilots survive, how on earth are the flocks of grounded chickens to avoid heart attacks from watching?"

To some in the movement, stunting makes no sense at all. To others, aerobatics is where it's at. E. M. Forster notes that humans are innately curious; "We are all like Scheherazade's husband in that we want to know what happens next." That helps to explain why Dix Erickson nearly drowned chancing a landing in the surf at Torrance (the Rogallo was destroyed). And why, to celebrate Leap Year, the Self-Soar Society one day launched 27 gliders simultaneously at Playa del Rey. And why, at 2,000 feet above Badwater, Death Valley, Rich Piccarelli detached from his Rogallo on purpose to become the first (insofar as is known) hang glider pilot to abandon a hang glider and land safely by parachute. And why Bob Wills took his grandmother flying in a Rogallo-built-for-two, and later flew a four-place craft fully loaded (plenty of leg room in coach). And why Burke Ewing frequently amuses his 65-pound best friend by taking it flying at Torrey, cradled in a sling. A German shepherd, part Airedale.

Alas, not all stunts are intentional. During a cross-country sampling of hang gliding sites from California to Michigan to Carolina, Reggie Miller of Berkeley was fascinated by a 2,000-foot hill near Winemucca, Nevada: "Nice shape, good landing area, paved road to the top, open to the public, and looked safe, because, like most Nevada mountains, it had no trees." Following a smooth morning flight, Miller paid small heed to drastic shifts in gusty wind. He launched into an adventure which he later described in *Wings of Rogallo* newsletter:

The buffeting started almost immediately and, thank God . . . I had built an extra-wide control bar. I was using every inch of it and ricocheted back and forth along its five-foot length several times a second just to maintain stability. Have you ever seen a small piece of paper in a turbulent wake

62

What to do till the wind gains strength? What pilots have always done: talk flying.

change its position several times up and down, 'round and 'round, in several seconds? That's what this ride was all about because I realized I was caught in the turbulent wake of a high wind spilling over the ridge to my right. Unfortunately, I gained altitude quickly and it took me a full minute before I could land on the ridge to my left and only half-way down the mountain. On the way down the kite downdrafted many times and so abruptly that I experienced free-fall, almost hitting my head on the keel boom and almost falling forward through the control bar, followed by sharp updrafting which strained the kite — over and over, again. It was real terror. The minute lasted an hour, and I quivered for five minutes. Ahhh, Mother Earth — kiss, kiss, kiss!

64

Competitive as well as curious, the new breed of bird meets in towering tournaments in nearly every region of the globe, save Russia, and if Astroturf now carpets a stadium in Moscow, the flapping of stressed Dacron soon may be heard along the River Don. Elsewhere, there are contests in the Austrian Alps, at the Kimberly Ski Area and elsewhere in British Columbia, off the storied green hills of England, in South Africa and Australia, and at a growing number of suitable sites in the United States.

At the first annual Sugarloaf (Maine) Hang Gliding Festival, some 70 contestants entered to compare their high altitude maneuvers, and luxuriate in a ski lift converted to the transportation of hang gliders and pilots. Other meets draw long lists of entries at Maine's Brodie Mountain, North Carolina's Kitty Hawk, and Michigan's Elberta Bluffs. Even flatland Kansans gather for an annual fly-off from a 150-foot hill near Lake Wilson Reservoir. Yet with so low a launchpad, Bill Frary of Denver in the most recent Kansas encounter polished the hillside for 7 minutes 39 seconds, an endurance record for the meet. Of Colorado's countless elevations created for foot-induced flights, perhaps best known is Telluride, with aerial rodeos performing from an 800-foot hill into a cattle pasture.

But it is in California where hang gliding competition is keenest. An annual meet at San Ysidro honors John J. Montgomery; another in Orange County is named for Francis M. Rogallo; still another occurs on the birthday, May 23, of Otto Lilienthal. Prizes for professional contests are climbing into the thousands of dollars.

At this writing there have been two national championships sponsored by the U.S. Hang Gliding Association. The first was at Sylmar, 24 miles northwest of downtown Los Angeles. Among the thirty invited pilots the favorites were Bob Wills, Pat Conniry, Kim Dawson, David Kilbourne and David Gibas. The field included two young California women, Carol Velderrain and Donnita Holland. The course descended from a peak in the Angeles National Forest to a landing area 1,200 feet below. In days shrouded by fog and brightened by sunshine, pilots were scored on turning ability, gracefulness of flight and safety and accuracy of landing. When all

In strong winds, for safety's sake, a kite is "wirelaunched" by an assistant holding cables near the nose.

66

*Maralys Wills is the mother of the
1975 American and Canadian hang gliding champions.*

the kites were back in their covers, Bob Wills had outflown all his rivals — all but his younger brother, Chris, 21. Chris scored 1,774 points out of a possible 2,000. "Only a bird," said one judge, "could have scored a perfect 2,000." Mike Larson of Golden, Colorado, gained third place in the inaugural nationals, and Terry Raymond of Santa Ana, California, placed fourth.

The 1974 nationals scheduled for late in the year at Escape Country, Trabuco Canyon, southeast of Los Angeles, were blown into 1975 by devil winds generated by fast-moving storm fronts. To an entry list of a hundred proven pilots were added fifty

openings to be won in preliminary competition. Courses designed for maximum skills in soaring, maneuvering through pylons, reaching the landing zone, and all-together landing were scored by a system that drastically penalized hot-dogging flight. In recognition of the inherent differences in flexible Rogallos and fixed-wing hang gliders, separate categories were provided.

Aside from a few scrapes and bruises, thumped helmets and one broken ankle in the preliminary heats, the national championships were completed without injuries. Some 800 flights departed hills of 500 and 1,500 feet of elevation, with demonstrations from four miles away, off the summit of Saddleback, 4,200 feet higher than the landing field. When the week of competition arrived at its final twilight, all the winners were Californians, in part, perhaps, because so many out-of-state entrants were obliged to depart before the weather improved. The order of finish for fixed-wing pilots was Jack Schroder, Redondo Beach, and Dave Cronk and Ron Richards, both of Torrance.

In flexible-wing competition, this time Bob Wills, Santa Ana, prevailed over brother Chris, who finished second. They were followed by Chris Price, Los Angeles; Chuck Nyland, South Laguna; Jerry Fenn,

*In a moment of triumph during
1975 United States nationals, Bob Wills is
congratulated by his brother and friend.*

Orange; Greg Mitchell, Mission Viejo; Roy Haggard, Visalia; David Muehl, Inglewood; Rich Finley, San Diego, and Mike Mitchell, Mission Viejo.

Nine out of the next ten finishers were also Californians. They were Trip Mellinger, Canoga Park; Dean Tanji, Santa Ana; John McVey, San Diego; Dave Saffold, Santa Barbara; Bob Skinner, San Diego; Mike Arrambide, Ventura; Charles Baughman, El Segundo; Tom Peghiny, Newton, Massachusetts; Patrick Hayes, Mission Viejo, and Bill Roberts, San Diego.

Good news and bad news emanates from flying sites. One pattern is all too familiar: As the sport arrives in a region, sites gain popularity, attracting the attention of authorities and property owners concerned about laws, regulations and accident liability. As flying permission is denied, the search moves on to other scenes, close in and far out.

In New Zealand Rick Poynter and Jeff Campbell have demonstrated how an 11-mile stretch of cliffs from Karioitahi to the Manukau Heads of Aukland can be flown nonstop, round trip. In the European Alps there are twenty or more mounts offering drops of 7,000 feet, and numerous drops of 2,000 feet, and many are served by cable cars or cog railways to lift hang gliders and pilots to takeoff areas.

70

In the eastern United States, depending on wind, both sides of Cape Cod are flyable. North Carolinians hang out at a 13-story-high sand dune called Jockey Ridge near where Orville and Wilbur did their thing in gliders. The Ozarks of Arkansas and Missouri cradle kite sites galore.

On the New York–Massachusetts border, Petersburg Pass boasts of a ski lift of 1,100 feet, and thermal and ridge soaring on most days. Another popular ski area is Nashoba, at Littleton, Massachusetts. Magic Mountain, Londonderry, Vermont, provides a 1,600-foot launch and lesser, beginner hills. Mount Washington, the highest elevation in New England, offering the greatest vertical drop east of the Rockies, was baptized in July, 1974, by Don McCabe. Notorious for swift weather changes which have claimed more than a hundred lives of skiers and climbers, Mount Washington, in New Hampshire, is recommended only for the most expert pilots. With nearly a mile of altitude to toy with, pilots have soared hang gliders there for as long as four hours.

New Mexico's Continental Divide . . . Michigan's Warren Dunes . . . Oregon's Cape Kiwanda . . . Colorado's ski parks . . . Arizona's Camelback Mountain and Shaw Butte . . . all are rivaled in the California motherland, where the majority of pilots

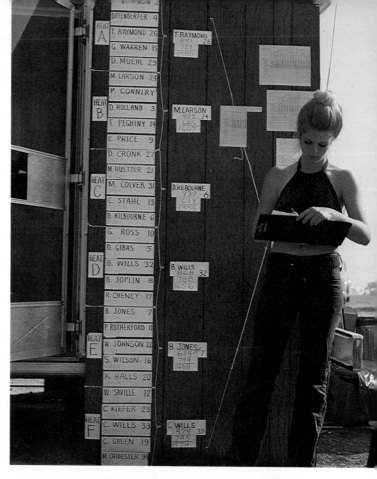

Action at the first national hang gliding championships in autumn, 1973, at Sylmar, California.

(thus far) dwell. At Palmdale, at San Clemente, at Malibu, at Crestline, at Palomar, at Thousand Oaks, at Little Mountain, at Point Fermin, hang gliders fly friendly skies. But efforts to open sites in public forests and parks have met with mixed success. One who winged it off Glacier Point in Yosemite alighted in the arms of rangers who judged the act to be "unnatural."

The bureaucratic revolving door entrapped Chris Price following his fabulous fling from Dantes View to the floor of Death Valley. Rangers forbade him from further flying, until he obtained a Special Use Permit, which Price then formally applied for. In due course, the chief ranger responded:

I am sorry, but we do not consider such use appropriate for a natural area within the National Park System, and your request

must be denied. Others areas exist near Death Valley that are suitable for your use and you may wish to give them careful consideration. We hold no prejudice against your chosen form of outdoor recreation, but find it distracting from the natural, historical, and scenic features for which Death Valley National Monument was established in 1933.

Disappointing the decision may be, the points are well made that other people, other pastimes, other philosophies flourished long before airspace filled with sibilant sails. Graceful, translucent wings — unpowered sailplanes and radio-controlled models — shared the lift above the storied palisades of Torrey Pines when the Rogallo glider wriggled into the NASA womb. Only by courteous cooperation and strict rules has Torrey remained open to hang gliders.

Elsewhere, alas, common sense and safety have been abandoned, to turn fabulous flings into bummers, hassles and the worst of bad trips.

Blessed by a sunset zephyr, John Dunham soars a ridge in a Windlord at Salt Creek, California.

You can't fly as good as the birds, Daddy, she said.
Oh yes, I can fly better than the birds.
You can't fly as high as the birds.
Yes. I can fly even higher than the birds.
You can't fly as fast as the birds.
Oh, I can fly much faster than any bird.
The child gave him a long, hard and furious look.
Well, you can't build a nest.

JOSEPH COLVILLE LINCOLN

5: *Homo Sapiens Volans*

THE NEW BREED DEFIES STANDARDIZATION. On some lanky skeletons lie the long, lean muscles of the swimmer-surfer. Chunkier builds betray converted sprinters. Skin pigmentation can range from ebony through copper through lemon to ivory. In both sexes, hair can be coarse and fine; long and short and black, colored or white. Some strut and preen like peacocks, while others waddle around as roughly feathered as molting mudhens.

A net cast over a gaggle of glider freaks ensnares the hatchling who knows he is immortal, along with the elderly buzzard whose own brittle wing has knit a fractured *humerus*. Some sing. Some guard their souls like half-lidded owls. The same flock will make a place for the middle-aged swinger clutching the sands of his youth so fiercely they trickle away more swiftly. The covey includes a chick so sexy, that even in gloves, flying denims, helmet, harness and boots, she fills sails with covetous sighs. Here is a poet. There, a pragmatist. Here, a scientist. There, a sensualist. Here, the doer. There, the philosopher. Yet for all of their differences they are bound by a kinship that transcends age and tongue and race and motivation and mentality.

. . . As birds, they fly.

"There are old pilots, and bold pilots, but no old, bold pilots." Volmer Jensen, born in 1909, and hang gliding's link to the past, lives not by luck but wits. That he still flies, hale and hearty, in the midst of his seventh decade, is a tribute to his willingness to accept expert advice, his impeccable craftsmanship and a penchant for folding up his wings when air

77

ditions are poor or unfavorable for flying.

Reed thin, tall and sharp-faced, Volmer says he acquired his blue eyes by staring at the sky. By "cut-and-try" designing in 1925 he fashioned his first glider. When private airplanes were banned from coastal zones during World War II, Volmer and Irv Culver flew around the regulations with their *So-Lo* rigid-wing biplane with rudder, elevator and ailerons. *So-Lo's* seven-to-one glide ratio enabled them to soar low hills near their San Fernando Valley homes. They were, of course, considered slightly daft.

Then, when all around them humans launched by foot into birdlike flight, they were inspired to create the *Swingwing* VJ-23. It, too, is a rigid wing with controls,

but a cantilevered monoplane. It weighs 100 pounds, flies at 16–25 mph, and from plans can be built with some $400 in materials in three months' spare time. Hundreds of times Volmer has entertained the bathers at El Segundo Beach by launching his *Swingwing* from a 35-foot, 23-degree dune with just two or three running steps, climbing, completing a series of figure-eight turns, and landing in two steps atop the dune. He does not hide his low opinion of flexible kites.

"When the wing deflates, there goes your lift," says Volmer.

Rogallo addicts respond that in all respect Volmer's bird is a simplified sailplane that's too heavy for one person to pack up a hill, requires 30 minutes to assemble, and another half hour to knock down.

As usual, Volmer has an answer. He says, "I have all the time of my life to devote to preparing for flight."

Burke Ewing III is 20. He dwells in an East San Diego subdivision in a ranchstyle house which has a rock band system sprawling over the entire living room, machine tools dominating the dining area, tubing and other materials utterly filling the garage, and water beds jiggling sensuously in the bedrooms. How many friends live with Burke on any given day

Manufacturer of Cal Gliders *is Dick Messina, left.*

is not always known to himself. The place is clean enough, although many walls sport bulletin boards and psychedelic signs, the most compelling of which (in the kitchen) in six-inch-high letters invites readers to carnally know housework. Burke is cool, funny, loyal, unorganized, free-spirited, chatty, and (he believes) poorly coordinated afoot. It is in the sky that he gets it all together. He flies every day he can. He will ignore appointments, lose money, neglect work — to fly.

Says he, "Couple of years ago I saw some dudes flying the cliffs, and I just had to do it. I went too fast. I mean, too fast. With only a few weeks of beach flying, one Sunday morning I took my folks out to Torrey when there wasn't a breath of wind and stepped off and went to the beach like a dying duck.

I was into flying only a few months when Jim Weir and me, and another guy, in September, 1973, we spent all night climbing to the top of Mount San Jacinto above Palm Springs. The peak is 10,830 feet above sea level and 2,000 feet of the granite rises above the top of the tram. The

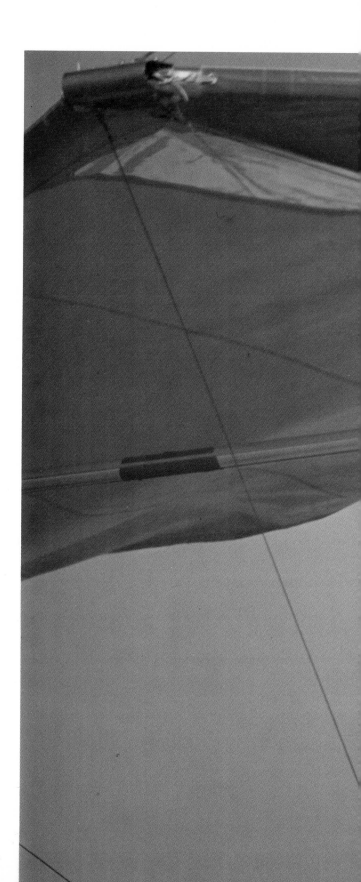

Windows in Reggie Jones' Dragonfly provide upward visibility.

80

Rich Finley, designer and hang glider test pilot, graduate of Annapolis, also flies Phantom fighter planes for the Navy.

and helped me hold it down and fold it. I had the shakes for an hour. And why not? I was up there an hour and twenty minutes in sheer terror.

Jim Weir's adventure, if anything, was scarier. Yet by whim the banshee winds chose to drop him into the center of Palm Springs, in front of a liquor store. Jim immediately went inside and bought a six-pack of beer and drank it.

climb was too much for one guy — he stashed his kite and helped us reach the peak.

Unreal, the way the wind was blowing. It was a fight to set up the kites. We were so stupid. We should never have launched. Once we were over the mountains the winds must have been gusting to 50 mph. I lost Jim right away. I climbed through the control bar and grabbed the front flying wires, and I still couldn't penetrate. I couldn't believe *the turbulence — like, 600 feet of downdrafting* right now, *and barely missing ridges. I hung in a steady gale for half an hour, and I said all sorts of things like, "Lord, if you'll let go of me, I'll do anything you ask," and somehow I got out of the mountains and over the desert, where the winds were* really *blowing. How I reached the desert floor I'll never know, and I still wasn't out of it. Luckily a couple of kids saw me trying to keep it on the ground, and they ran a quarter of a mile*

82

John Dunham, world class pilot in Austrian, Canadian and American competition.

At 20, Tom Peghiny is an executive in a glider company.

"We were so ignorant," says Burke. "That kind of flying should never happen again."

In his home town of Kirkland, Washington, Dick Gammon is known as a mature real estate broker in his early 30s whose diversions range from skiing to skydiving to hang gliding. He was, in 1970, among the first to fly in the Northwest. His early glider was home-built of irrigation tubing,

from Eipper plans. Few have been more active in club organizaton, accident reporting, safety promotion.

Of late, he wonders whether flying is part of his future.

I'm still interested in the sport. I don't know of another activity that brings together a greater variety of ages and occupations and social standing: housewives and doctors and hippies and teenagers and

Chris Wills, hang gliding's first national champion.

83

radicals and members of the Establishment. In that sense, hang gliding is most democratic.

My current problem is that at the degree of skill where I am now, I simply do not much enjoy climbing to the top of a little hill and gliding down and walking back up only to glide down again. I want to soar. And I know how to do that safely at certain sites which are dangerous for those of lesser skills.

That's what is worrying me. Is it in my best interests, and the interests of my fellow man, to fly so well where I do? Do others watch me and push themselves too fast? Why won't they pay heed to verbal admonishments? What are my responsibilities if others are led into trouble? So these days I am proceeding very, very slowly, and thinking a great deal. . . .

For some, hang gliding is a together trip. It is the style of Bob and Robin Skinner of San Diego, an inordinately handsome couple whose air base is a firm named Flight Realities. Friends call Bob, "Father Flight," and Robin, "Mother Reality."

They both were into sport parachuting and wondering if the sky held a higher high, when Ted Webster, who had learned from Dave Kilbourne, explained some of the basics of Rogallo handling to Bob, at Playa del Rey.

"No one really knew that much in those days about pilot training," recalls Bob. "Every small lesson had to be learned from experience, often with some accompanying pain. It took me six weeks of beach flying to gain much control over the kite. Knowing what I know now, those problems could have been avoided."

Bob has instructed 500 others in hang gliding, and although the educational process is more efficient, he has second thoughts about some of his graduates: "It's almost too easy now. After a few weeks on the beach at Cantamar some students become pretty good and right away they want to go fly off some mountains. That's too big a step, from the dunes to Elsinore."

Still the great majority of Skinner's pupils advance no farther than the beach scene — low altitude skimming over sand. It is the quiet, reasonably safe side of the sport that is lost in sensational reporting. Yet as governments take away relatively safe flying sites, fliers are left with the unsafe. In this regard state and local authorities are more of a threat to low-key enjoy-

84

falling — and you hold hands and kiss. It was like that the first time we flew gliders together at Sylmar. Bob went first, and I was a bit delayed, and I thought I had lost him, but when I turned over a ridge, there he was soaring back to me, and the sky was ours in a fantastic closeness."

Commitment. That is Joe Faust's own word for his relationship with hang gliding, and it is an understatement. His defiance of gravity seems born in him.

In his day as a high jumper he was the best of his age in the nation — 6 feet, 8

ment of hang gliding than is the federal government.

Of the thousands of accomplished pilots, few are women, and Robin's explanation may hold the key: "You have to be physically aggressive to launch. I don't mean big, strong or totally athletic. You have to take command of yourself and your kite and then take command of the world around you. The capacity for physical aggression in our society is more developed among males than females, and women tend to be timid with the kite, which results in failure and discouragement. I think I kept in training because as a parachutist I knew how beautiful the end results could be."

Which are? "There's an unforgettable moment in sport parachuting — that first time you find one another when you are

86

A founder of the Professional Flyers Association, John McVey.

A leading test pilot in his mid-teens, Mike Mitchell.

inches at 15 years, 7 feet, 2 inches in junior college and 7 feet, 4¾ inches in practice. He was off his feed for the 1960 Olympics in Rome, and then the time came for the former student body president voted most-likely-to-succeed to begin climbing the corporate ladder as an industrial engineer for McDonnell-Douglas.

Somewhere about Rung Four, Joe met a hang glider down on the beach, picked it up, and gave it his heart. He wrote a lengthy memo to his superiors explaining why a gigantic aerospace firm in the late 1960s should establish a department of research and development of foot-launched aircraft and put Joe Faust in charge. Joe Faust's deadline passed, and Joe went away from there.

Since, he has dedicated his life to hang gliding. The subsistence he has eked as founder-president of the Self-Soar Association has varied from marginal to minimal. With his wife he makes a home at Venice. Although Joe's *Hang Glider Weekly* more accurately should be named the *Occasionally,* the journal and its technical sister, *Low & Slow,* testify to the determination of one man to keep all lines of communication open within an experimental sport.

Tolerance. There is another word that goes with Faust. His columns are open to every responsible voice. Sacrifice. Joe does

88

Jim Schumaker.

not vibrate to that term. "My seventeen years of avoiding gravity have consumed every physical, mental and occupational ounce of my being — a grand experience." Commercial. This word Joe equates with trouble. When the sport consists of humans and gliders, the usual result is beautiful. But when the third, commercial, element is present, when for money people are pressed to try to excel, too often the outcome is a bummer. So believes Joe Faust, committed.

Being generally lighter in weight, the women who fly hang gliders must follow a separate set of rules. They may launch in less wind, and soar in less lift. Conversely, they may not possess the strength and poundage to cope with winds ideal for 200-pound men.

Only one in a hundred pilots is female, but they who master self-flight add a dimension beyond mere numbers. Kathy Stewart, coed. Joanne Faust, Joe's wife. Karen Cronk and Joy Lovejoy, wives of glider manufacturers. Darlene Allard, mother of three, who helped her husband, Don, build family kites. Carol Velderrain, daughter of Russ, pioneer glider maker. Janet Seagars, mother of grown children, kindergarten teacher, sailplane enthusiast. Jackie Metz, 105 pounds sensationally arranged. Ester Gail Escovedo, three years aloft. Katie and Ro Lambie, sisters. Clara E. Allen, registered nurse.

Chris Talbot-Jones built an *Icarus II* with the help of his wife, Vickie. "He encourages me to grow in any direction I can, even if it is on male stomping ground. It's one of the things I appreciate about him greatly." But the sport imposes special duties on a pilot who is also a woman, mother, wife, sandwichmaker, medic, and minister to male egos.

As she says, "Our frustration has been that the wind stops blowing when we arrive and commences when we leave. It's a hassle getting a whole family together (including two small boys), mounting the glider, putting it together at the site, paci-

89

fying the kids and finding that the wind just died down."

Down Under the kiwi flies, using the alias of William Moyes, operator of a successful electrical engineering firm in Sydney, Australia. Moyes has done it all. These days he sells flexible wings to his fellow Aussies, citing these credentials.

— Likely his experience is the longest and most varied of modern Rogallo hang glider pilots.

— In 1967 he became the first to exceed a thousand feet of altitude, over Tuggerah Lake, by boat tow. The next year he tied himself to a 10,000-foot-long wire cable, and rose to 2,870 feet on Lake Ellesmere in New Zealand.

— As early as 1968 Moyes was skiing off heights, notably Mount Crackenback in the Australian Alps for a flight of a mile and a half.

— Moyes' descent of Grand Canyon was precisely as planned. At 6:30 a.m., July 19, 1970, he astounded South Rim tourists by plunging over a vertical cliff, gliding 8 minutes 32 seconds, and landing 4,800 feet lower, at America's most remote resort, Phantom Ranch.

— In a kite strengthened for high speed, on October 18, 1971, at Amery, Wisconsin, Moyes was towed up behind a *Super Cub* to an altitude of 8,610 feet.

Strangely, he has never received credit and fame worthy of his deeds, perhaps because of his self-effacing ways. Of the birdlings of the 1970s Moyes says, "You blokes are making such progress now, it's hard for an old bloke like me to catch up."

When he wrote *Darius Green and His Flying Machine* a century ago John Townsend Trowbridge envisioned something of the real-life Taras Kiceniuk, Jr. Before he

Dean Tanji, master of the Wills Wing.

The Arrambide twins, Mike and David.

scientific and moral support of his father, also a glider pilot, young Taras fashioned a tailless biplane with wingtip rudders. *Icarus I* achieved controlled, soaring flight in October, 1971, but structural weakness was revealed when in a ground-skimming accident soon afterward, the wings crumpled into a pile of styrofoam, plastic film, aluminum and baling wire.

Icarus II succeeded — a biplane so strong and well designed that it quickly advanced from seashore dunes to mountain

was old enough to vote, Taras had acquired a worldwide notoriety among hang gliding enthusiasts. Now in his 20s, his aura of legend is such that crowds of spectators collect where he flies, and at meets, with electric swiftness the news spreads:

"Hey, Taras just arrived."

Taras. The first name is enough, although actually there are two of them. The senior Taras is an engineer and administrator of the famed Palomar Observatory in Southern California. The younger Kiceniuk contributed most to hang gliding while a student at California Institute of Technology.

Following some early, imperfect adventures with Rogallos, Taras decided that rigid-wing configurations (*a la* Lilienthal, Chanute, the Wrights, Jensen, Lambie, Miller) promised better performance. With

Someday from a balloon? — Larry Witherspoon.

92

Stephen McCarroll, in those foolish days before he
learned to fly with a helmet that saved his life.

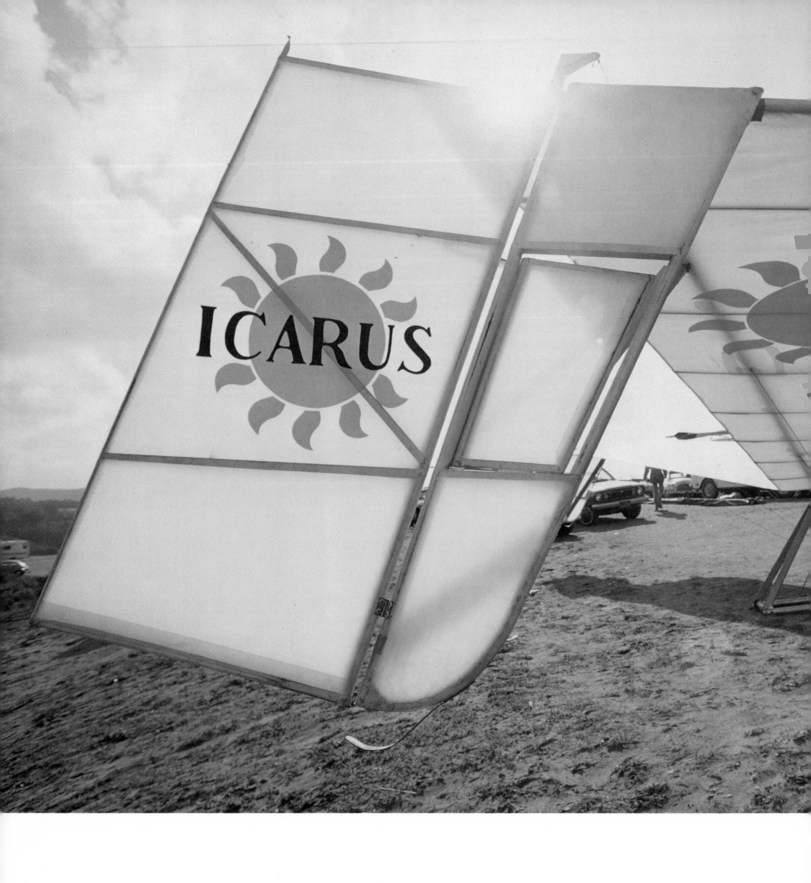

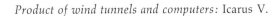
Product of wind tunnels and computers: Icarus V.

ridge soaring and ocean cliffs. By now there is *Icarus V*, a monowing sans tail, with pronounced sweep and dihedral, 32 feet in span and 65 pounds complete. Taras speaks glowingly of its capabilities: stall speed of 16 mph, top speed of 60 mph in still air, rudders that operate independently and can be used as dive brakes. The shape of *V's* wing was determined by an electronic computer, as explained in a paper given at the AIAA/SSA/MIT International Symposium on the Technology and Science of Low Speed and Motorless Flight in September, 1974.

Still, brown-haired, brown-eyed, slender Taras is no precocious stuffed shirt. He told a reporter from *Smithsonian:* "Look at it this way: It can't be any more scary for us than it is for a baby bird whose wings aren't even *ready*, for god's sake." And, "It's a *kick* to hang glide. You're all alone up there, not enclosed in a cockpit like you are in a sailplane, but out in the open. That has to be the closest thing to bird flight. It *has* to be. Just you and the wind in the wires."

95

6: The Crashingest Crashing

THE DAY IS A PAGE RIPPED FROM THE BROCHURE of a Southern California chamber of commerce. A midwinter zephyr, perfumed by chaparral, presses across the toast-brown mesas. Through tattered swatches of vanishing cumulus, the sun casts a warm, golden net over the western flanks of the Santa Ana Mountains. Feathered tribes fleeing the ice of Alaska, Alberta and Dakota fill the hardwood canyons with song.

A day to climb a cliff. Or catch a "stokah-bokah" curl off San Clemente. Or run with a *Hobie Cat* down Mission Bay. Or drink some wine. Or make some love. Or fly.

Fred D. Smith, Jr., a telephone cable splicer from Long Beach, is adept at piloting his hang glider in the seat harness, but is inexperienced in flying it prone. Needing practice for the nationals, he now launches in a prone harness off the 500-foot level into a problem of some complexity. He must turn a pylon, cross a target of concentric chalked circles as low and slow as he dares, drop a balloon water bomb, and proceed to another target for landing.

Fred's a husky dude, and he kills a lot of altitude maneuvering his 20-foot sail around the pylon. With good airspeed he moves into the bombing range. Electing to get lower, Fred turns *downwind*. Fred is aware that although his groundspeed may now increase, his airspeed may drastically decrease. But at this moment his awkwardness with the unfamiliar harness compounded by his fiddling with the balloon delivers Fred Smith to the Hard Knocks School of Applied Physics.

He loses flying speed at forty feet of altitude.

His right wing stalls; sideslipping, man and kite accelerate to the baked ground with a

pitiful thump and a huge geyser of dust. The wings, like those of an enormous, gorgeous moth in throes of death, quiver, sag and come to rest. Stunned but functioning, Fred detaches his harness and rolls away from the still-dangerous wreckage. Friends rush to him.

"You okay, man?" asks a fellow pilot.

"I'm alive, I guess. That stupid, goddam balloon."

The profanity informs Fred's friends that Fred is still himself. They are relieved.

"You really fucked it up this time, Fred," says a handsome young woman who walks with a limp and whose left wrist, elbow and shoulder are encased in a solid cast.

"You want out of your harness, man?"

"Yeah, but be careful with that left ankle. I think the sonofabitch is busted."

"You pretty sure?"

"I know goddam well. Stupid balloon."

(Toward the hangar) "Call rescue! He broke something."

"I gigged it when I took my hand off the control bar to drop that stupid balloon."

"Don't go into shock, Fred."

"You want we should cut your pants and shoe off?"

"I hear the sheriff's siren, Fred. You got anything in your pockets you don't want the fuzz to find?"

Crashing can be painful, but for the onlooker there is also out-of-focus beauty.

In an uncharacteristically awkward moment,
an experienced pilot in an advanced, high-performance
kite stalls a wing on landing.

Fred grins wryly. Pats pockets. Shakes head.

Soon the medics arrive to bind the break in a cardboard splint. Fred declines the expense of an ambulance ride, choosing instead to drink some beer while a buddy transports him to the hospital in a truck. A few days later he is back in the Santa Ana hills — in a wheelchair.

"The ball-and-socket's all screwed up," says Fred. "I guess I'll have to wait a while before I can fly again, and, *O hell yes* I want to fly again, although the docs say that even with an artificial ankle I might never regain more than 50 percent use of the foot."

At that, Fred Smith might consider himself blessed. For a gross violation of the laws of gravity, he received a comparatively light sentence. For all too many other hang glider pilots, transgressing Sir Isaac Newton's axiom of $F = ma$ has resulted in capital punishment. The reasons range from misfortune through research through poor judgment through inferior execution to malfunction. The realities involve velocities of 50 mph and greater, and the vulnerability of human anatomy.

Inevitable? Jonathan Livingston Seagull to Fletcher Lynd Seagull: "We don't tackle flying through rock until a little later in the program." Confucius: "To make a mistake and not correct it is to make another mistake." Tommy Prothro: "Luck, I define as the product of design."

Bobby Kennedy, Ed Gardia, Verl Gleed, Mark Peterson, Ron David. They were among the first casualties. A tow rope would snap or wind would change or an intermediate pilot would be unaware that while learning 360-degree turns he could lose 300 feet of altitude in a matter of seconds.

Exhibitionists, the Sizemore brothers of Westminster, California, bet their lives as the Flying Circus that the Rogallo wing could be deliberately stalled to produce a vertical dive from which recovery could be effected without fail. No one who saw them pull out of dives a few feet above the ground ever will forget. Nor will those at Sylmar in November, 1973, when, during such a dive, the sail of the wing of David, 20, inverted and rapidly decelerated. Now from above David's body at 65 mph plunged into the frame, collapsing the keel and a leading edge. He did not survive.

Nor did Chuck Kocsis, Dave Gibas, James Foster, and Eric Wills, all victims of imperfect turns. Gary Smith of Las Vegas, Nevada, lost his life when his kite col-

lapsed under tow and Thomas Williamson, of San Jose and flying at Daly City, was electrocuted when he dropped into a 12,000-volt power line. For 1974 it was an inauspicious beginning.

"What is happening?" asked Editor Joe Faust in his *Hang Glider Weekly*. Joe had been in the movement almost from genesis, and abruptly the vision of sand beaches, bikinis and belly-slides was transformed into a montage of paralysis, plaster casts and obituaries. Into Joe's news bureau poured reports of fatalities in New Zealand, Rhodesia, Brazil, England, Australia, Canada, France.

"Thousands more people are now with a wing," wrote Joe, "and without adequate skill and knowledge." He called for "wisdom in training and practice, courage in commercial design (by holding back a non-proven modification until fully understood). Users of the wing ought to realize by now that no one who dares the rough winds can have a good bet. A strong wing is not enough; it must have adequate aerodynamic characteristics and be flown in weather that speaks sanely of the pilot."

Yet, more died: James Phillips, Steven Ervin, and Donald Walen, 17, observed standing in his control bar. Losses from which the sport of hang gliding could not learn were doubly tragic. The lesson for which Doug DeYoung paid so dearly was that aircraft pilots of great experience are not immune; indeed, their conventional reflexes may be their undoing. DeYoung, an airline captain and intermediate hang

glider pilot, was flying off Barrs Mountain near Seattle in perfect conditions with a superior wing. Working with 2,000 feet of altitude, DeYoung completed two 360-degree turns, entered a mild stall, then immediately went into a hammerhead stall which induced a vertical dive to the ground. Washington's first hang gliding fatality may have been the victim of the aircraft pilot's impulse "to push the stick forward to get the nose down" — the opposite control required for a hang glider.

With television cameras grinding, an unwise pilot does the movement no good by stalling out at 50 feet while trying to turn downwind, crunching nose first to a knockout crash which draws a crowd to revive him.

Not all accidents were fatal, and from the emergency wards came word that a lot of little factors are critical in Rogallo flight. Norris White (fractured hip and pelvis) advised against launching at Zuma Beach north of Los Angeles in winds exceeding 30 mph. Despite his crawling halfway through his control bar to depress his nose, he kept climbing, then flew straight backward to crash keel first. Bret Humphries (broken knee cap) knocked a plug of mud from his aft keel tube, moved his swingline a mere two inches forward, and launched off Saddleback. The combination of two small weight changes moved the center of gravity so far forward that all his strength was consumed in pushing out to sustain level flight, and he arrived at the landing zone seven minutes later, too exhausted to control his landing.

Jeff Jobe (fractured pelvis, leg), famous in advertisements and magazine articles, hooked a ski into an obstacle on takeoff in the Grand Tetons. Mike Koman (shattered wrist and ribs), didn't know when he was well off. He plopped into a Pennsylvania tree — unharmed — extricated himself from his harness, reached for a branch, missed, and fell like Newton's apple.

Bob Konigsor (broken wrist) thought he was progressing nicely with his sixth flight at Sorrento Valley when one wing struck a fence post. Brian Stevens (broken leg) at Palos Verdes had a wing give way at 400 feet, yet he spiraled it down, to live. Hang gliding cost Will Battles, 60, an inch of height (fused vertebrae) as the result of landing hard on his butt at Pismo Beach during gusty winds. After more than two years in the sport, Battles gave it up.

Harley Lester. Bruce Slingerland. Fred Espey. Patrick Loren. Mystery shrouds certain aspects of all their deaths, yet none so romantically as that of Roger Staub who dived in from 450 feet at Verbier, Switzerland. The winner of the Olympic giant slalom race at Squaw Valley in 1960 was reported by friends to have been depressed in spirits. *Sports Illustrated* commented: "In Roger's case, the mood was accompanied by a compulsive reading of the novel *Jonathan Livingston Seagull* by Richard Bach, a story about a gull who would not be held within conventional bounds of normal gull flying habits. The hero of the book found a new and radiant incarnation after plunging into a seaside cliff after he miscalculated a headlong high-speed dive. As Bach wrote, 'He could fly higher and it was time to go home.' "

Robert N. (Pete) Rutherford, Washington. William Shultz, Kansas. Timothy Eldridge, California. Francis McConnell, Arizona. To Joe Gilmaker of Garden Grove came the dubious distinction of fatally crashing an *Icarus II*, a rigid-wing hang glider generally considered a super stable design — in the hands of experts. Joe was

104

a beginner in the biplane, and he complicated his final flight by testing a new seat. Motion picture film by an amateur photographer suggests that attempts to use the seat produced a dive which threw Joe forward, a position which became impossible to change, and Little Mountain became the biggest mountain the lad would ever fly.

Elsewhere, the toll continued. Julian Fitch. Michael LeBrun. Bruce McCosh. Carl Burman. Jeffrey Miller. Nancy Jo Whilldin became hang gliding's first female fatality. Big Southern Butte, rising 2,456 feet above an Idaho desert claimed the life of Jerry Randall, 31, professional stuntman. An accident review concluded that he ignored several safety rules by flying alone, flying in strong gusty winds, and launching with wing loading too light for conditions. Then, Paul Horn. Greg Lorinca. And ominously, Lloyd Short, 30. Short was a championship class pilot and television performer. Also at Big Southern Butte, his kite disassembled at 2,000 feet. Alas, an assembly pin which might have kept it all together was found later in Lloyd's pocket.

A consensus holds that Sean Quinn caught the Big Thermal at Point Fermin because he tried a 360-degree turn while ridge soaring where all turns should be figure eights *away from the ridge*. Was Bill

Taylor wearing glasses when he launched into fog off Canada's Mount Hope to honor an exhibition agreement? He became that nation's first fatality. William Grainger, Peter Johann, Lynn Christensen, Chris Paton. The tragic roster lengthened into Autumn, 1974. In quick succession, three deaths shocked the hang gliding movement. These were not fledglings testing their newfound pinions in beginning flights, but on any given day perhaps the three keenest pilots in the world.

• Pat Conniry, 24, top-seeded in the 1973 invitational nationals, had flown more varieties of hang gliders than anyone else. At Big Tujunga Mountain, in brisk winds, from 1,000 feet Pat's modified Rogallo dived without recovery to the earth.

• Curt Stahl, 15, professional test pilot of unsurpassed instinct, coordination and skill. At Elsinore, in mild steady air, the third of a series of intentional low altitude porpoising maneuvers deflated Curt's experimental sail and led to a 30-mph crash and fatal brain damage.

• John Hughes, 22, whose reputation for aerial achievement was rivaled only by his casual approach to safety. He had set a world's endurance record in Hawaii using an old, much-crashed kite mended with a length of broomstick handle. Fate abandoned him on an Oahu cliff when he im-

properly hung a borrowed seat. Airborne, when he encountered strong lift, webbing stitches parted, allowing John to fall free from his kite 500 feet.

Louis Sendledorfer. John Kaufman. Scott Trumble. George Tye. Ross Swernemann. Steve Williams. Fred Coleman.

"Steve McCarroll very well might have been the next on that list," said Steve Mc-Carroll. He spoke with difficulty, his concentration interrupted by the throbbing of his right leg. An incision angrily scribed the outside of that thigh, which now concealed a knee-to-hip steel pin holding the three pieces of his femur more or less together. He was somewhat slower of speech because of medication, and (he thought) from loss of blood. Two units of plasma were on the way.

"Valentine's Day," said Steve. "Torrey was really cookin'. Wind conditions were ideal for advanced flying: right out of the southwest squarely against the cliff. I'd been flying seated for two years and prone two and a half months, and my confidence and skills were improving. I set up my nineteen-seventeen Rogallo, carefully checked out the harness. I felt ready to fly.

It was one of my best days ever — 15 or 20 minutes of cranking turns and getting

unbelievable lift. We all know that usually when Torrey is best for flying the rotor (curling downdraft) on top is most treacherous. From a height of about 200 feet above the top of the cliff I made a normal approach downwind, then turned upwind to land. Despite the distracting activity of a dog and spectators below, and a gust that popped me up 20 feet, I sorted it all out and touched down like I was landing on cotton. I even drew some applause.

So after resting, and making minor adjustments to my harness, which had been hurting my back, I launched again. I flew for about 10 minutes. There were about a half-dozen kites in the air and a couple of rigid wings. I was really beginning to get the feel of turns, and I was handling my pitch control really well. Again, with an altitude 200 feet higher than the cliff I was flying southward when straight ahead and at the same altitude another kite was bearing down on me. I know the standard maneuver is to pass on the right, but the other kite had me pinned against the cliff, and the way things were developing, I had no assurance that if I crossed in front of him over the beach, he wouldn't turn left, and we'd have a head-on.

I estimate the other kite influenced me to move about five feet more than I wished to go toward the cliff. That was all it took to

This man needs a nurse who is also skilled in mending clothes and repairing hang gliders.

put me in the rotor. The sails deflated. In the couple of seconds I had I became aware of terrific speed and loss of altitude. I fought to get turned around into the wind but had no lift in the sails, and in the last instant I tried to throw forward into a violent flare.

That likely saved my life. Witnesses estimate the kite went straight in at 50–55 mph, but my body was sideways, and my leg made a pretzel out of itself and the control bar before I crunched in on my shoulder, which luckily was covered by two shirts and two jackets.

109

Breaking the leg saved my life. That, and the helmet. Even with the helmet I was knocked unconscious — and didn't come around until I was on the X-ray table. Without the helmet, there's no doubt the next name on the list would have been mine.

Stephen confessed that in his moment of truth he possibly possessed one option for avoiding a head-on collision, or the merciless rotor.

"Assuming that the other pilot would maintain altitude — and I had no reason to believe he would — I might have tucked it in and dived for the beach."

Few pilots want to waste time and energy climbing back up the tortuous trail to the top of Torrey. But if Stephen had had that choice he could have squandered a year. That's how long doctors said would pass before he could walk normally again.

A narrow escape from the Big Thermal: the pilot of this broken kite on Palomar Mountain chose not to fly questionable lift over a 1,000-foot ledge, and instead landed without injury in a tree.

*A lively curiosity has spread among all classes of thinking people
as to the names of the birds they see, what they feed on, and
something of their coming and going. . . . Not only are our
birds protected, but unusual opportunity has been given to study them.
The advance field work, coupled with the constant improvement
in photography, has obtained results little short of astounding.*

BIRDS OF AMERICA, 1917

7: Birds of No Feathers

WHAT CAN A BIRDWATCHER include in his report on *Homo sapiens volans?* Has this newly evolved form of class Aves, now available for every bird fancier's life list, existed long enough to establish distinct traits? Field notes, subspecies *H.s.v. americanus:*

COMMON NAME — Hang glider pilot.

OTHER NAMES — Sky surfer, Flexible wing flier, Kite Freak, Sky Sailor, Hot Dog.

DESCRIPTION — Length, 60–75 inches (with exceptions); weight, 85–210 pounds (more or less). Adult male breeding plumage, knit suits and body shirts of all colors; flying plumage, helmeted crown, body of denim and funky flash; eclipse plumage, prenuptial molt accelerates in spring and later may be observed totally devoid of plumage in public and private locations. Adult female breeding plumage, double-breasted see-throughs and flowing robes; flying plumage, helmeted crown, tee shirts of astonishing scenes, Levi's, sneakers; eclipse plumage, cutoffs and string bikinis, trending to nude when males are molting. Immature occurrences of this subspecies is more revealed by actions than plumage.

NEST — Mostly urban pads, a high percentage near schools, colleges and universities. Nesting materials often include poster displays of species types, technical journals discussing lift/drag ratios, sink rates and wing chords, hang gliding decals, and an assortment of tangs, Nico sleeves, turnbuckles, pop rivets and wing nuts.

GENERAL RANGE — First introduced to coastal dunes of California (disputed). Now breeds from Mount McKinley, Alaska, to Long Island, New York, and southward beyond Baja California and Rio de Janiero. Extremely migratory in all seasons by incorporating

*No indoor, caged bird, the hang glider sportsman;
because by definition it is an outdoor, ideally
mountain-seeking activity, a unique lifeway come into
being, combining camping, partying, sunbathing and
when the wind is cooking — flying.*

every means of transportation, primarily automobiles designed to carry folded wings. Originally this subspecies walked between flights; now tends to prefer to ride, often in vans which also serve as mobile nests. Related species now worldwide, although no sightings confirmed in Red China, Antarctica and Central Sahara.

HAUNTS AND HABITATS — Mating is not always for life. Difficult to determine which sex is the aggressor. Courting antics most bizarre of all life: gamut of swaggering, coy wing-dragging, drumming. As far

For some families, hang gliding is a togetherness trip.

A birdling for the 1985 nationals.

as is known, mating has never occurred in flight. In daily life, subspecies is gregarious and at times argumentative. Reluctant to fold wings, particularly at national meets. Constantly watches other birds of all kinds for clues to keener flight. Seldom seen in singles; often in flocks.

Voice — Most accomplished of all birds. Can yodel like the yellow-billed loon, cackle like the Cooper's hawk, gobble like the turkey, hoot like the spruce grouse, whistle like the bobwhite, squawk like the great blue heron, trumpet like a whooping

Ground school today is thought to be a must in hang gliding training, and some flight schools employ a flight simulator such as this to instruct beginners in the basic shifts of weight on which Rogallo control depends.

crane, peep like a black oystercatcher, trill like the buff-breasted sandpiper, rasp like the Eastern kingbird, twitter like the barn swallow, squeak like the starling and warble like the purple finch. Although no audiospectrograms are published, numerous tapes are available. The meaning of the calls usually have something to do with (1) the wind, (2) flying theory and (3) sites open or closed to hang gliding.

FEEDING — Will eat and drink almost anything, although because of remoteness of flying sites, the subspecies is thought to be adapting rapidly to a diet of stale sandwiches and hot wine. When given choices *H.s. americanus* prefers cheeseburgers and Coors beer. Also partial to seeds, nuts, fruits, vegetables, and baked goods.

118

*Radical evolution has taken place in harnesses;
in this type arranged for prone flight,
comfort is increased with sheepskin padding.*

*The love/hate feelings which pilots hold
for their helmets is based on the loss of hearing wind,
yet helmets are proven lifesavers, and increasingly,
pilots are using them.*

119

120

Hang gliding's acceptance into the American culture is established by the proliferating graffiti it inspires.

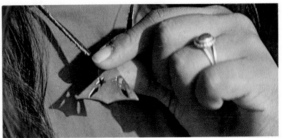

At first glance, a gathering of flexible kites could be mistaken for the temporary encampment of a colorful caravan inspired by Khayyam.

122

Not yet as organized as the Audubon Society, hang gliding spectators are growing in numbers and appreciation of pilot skills, and they provide an element which cannot reach the ears of other aircraft fliers: resounding applause.

Accompanying new freedoms of flight among gliding enthusiasts are the unfettered lifestyles of a generation rebelling against old-fashioned hang-ups.

8: Another Endangered Species?

FOR ALL THEIR SCIENCE, ENERGY AND ADROITNESS, gliding enthusiasts in the main are hopeless romanticists, eccentrics and elitists. Their view of life is through a prism uniquely their own, and in their eyes their act looms marvelous and magnified. The antipathy of violent, commercial team sports, ultralight flight reserves its ultimate rewards for intense, personal experience. And so it is that many participants are nonbelongers, and others, even among membership of their organizations, stand apart. In trade publications and newsletters, at business meetings and flying exhibitions, pilots and friends often agree to disagree.

It is a cell of democracy that might have earned the praise of Robert Frost: "The best things and best people rise out of their separateness; I'm against a homogenized society because I want the cream to rise."

But in a society that seems hell-bent for homogenization, to be independent is to be vulnerable. Along with constructive criticism, threats of regulation and volumes of positive and negative publicity, hang gliding has attracted a host of born enemies. Their reasoning follows a formula: hang gliding serves no practical purpose; as recreation it is dangerous; people must be protected from their own folly; surely there ought to be some laws to discourage the riding of kites.

Politicians, editorial writers and self-appointed defenders of the public weal have furthered this theme within a populace inured to regimentation. The legitimacy of hang gliding has been questioned, on grounds of safety and sanity, by newspapers. They are the same publications which provide prominent space for boxing matches that leave the

127

brains of fighters permanently damaged. They are the same papers which accept advertising from a sport whose climax is the extraction of opponents' teeth with hockey sticks. They are the same periodicals which glorify and promote high-speed car races that pollute the air, waste energy and endanger spectators as well as drivers. Thus far at least, the sport of hang gliding has not wiped out the first ten rows of fans at Turn Four.

Another sort of press, unguarded in approval, may have hurt the pastime of hang gliding even more than the detractors. There have been far too many superficial television treatments extolling rapturous flight for Everyman. Too many feature writers have skimmed once across the beach to write a story headed, "Now, *everybody* can fly." Wolfgang Langewiesche and the editors of *Reader's Digest* somehow should be made to eat the crow published in February, 1974: "If you want to fly, really fly, there's a new way now, open to all. All you need is a super-simple, super-cheap device called a Rogallo Wing — sort of a sail spread over a few metal poles. Tote it to the nearest grassy hill or dune on the beach, unfold it, start running downhill against the wind, raise the front edge a little so that the air gets underneath, and off you sail into the wild blue yonder.

129

"And that's *all*. . . ."

Fortunately, *all* Americans do not believe everything they read, but such simplistic advice, disseminated through a circulation of 13 million, surely generated unwanted business for the emergency wards. In fact, the super-simple, super-cheap Rogallos of the beginning years of necessity were crafted by owners, usually gifted tinkerers, with sparse data. An estimated 10,000 plans for gliders were sold — 4,000 of a Chanute-type glider by Jack Lambie — and the products generally were safe for ground skimming and low altitude dunes flights.

But high performance and advanced maneuvers called for more expensive materials and manufacturing, which now impose a base price of $600–$800 upon a reliable, well designed and properly tuned Rogallo. And just as many human specimens lack the judgment, strength and coordination for climbing trees, riding bicycles and skipping across streams on slippery rocks, they likewise are unsuited for brotherhood with the wind.

All that said, hang gliding has been criticized fairly from without and within the movement. As the sport surged into the 1970s the early birds went aloft in some incredibly inferior craft: furniture tubing, playground swingseats, plastic sails, baling

wire, so poorly engineered and wrought that it was a miracle they ever got up and down.

In those days, too, manufacturers multiplied like fruit flies. The survival rate also was similar. For a while it was as if five out of ten new pilots founded a factory. (The other five opened flying schools, or as Lloyd Licher once observed, "Men who have flown twice are writing manuals.") Designs of leading kitemakers were freely copied and marketed under freshly minted brand names. In a classic turnabout, a newcomer borrowed a kite design, improved on it, only to have the original manufacturer adopt the improved design in his own new model.

Early on, it became clear that there would not be *one*, perfect Rogallo, for all kinds of flight, conditions of air, and degrees of pilot ability. As a rule, modifying the standard Rogallo for high performance resulted in a loss of stability: "The *Piper Cub* as compared to a jet fighter." As in the larger world of aviation, all hang gliders were found to have limitations; some were chancy in high bank turns; all are structurally weak without kingposts; some of the rigid-wing gliders are not suited for pulling Gs in stressful maneuvers. In a recall remindful of the automobile industry, the manufacturer of 200 copies of one

Negotiating a shallow turn is a new model Dragonfly *designed by Roy Haggard and developed by Pete Brock.*

high-performance kite publicly advertised a willingness to restore its products to a more stable, standard Rogallo design. At the same time the company claimed that accidents with the wing, which it likened to a high-performance sports car, were "related to either poor judgment, poor flying conditions, unfamiliarity with the sail's performance, or poor tuning, resulting in sustained dives and slips."

Although less than two years in formation, the Hang Glider Manufacturers Association is leading the way to the excellence of design and construction found in general, commercial and military aviation. HMA minimum specifications are detailed to nuts, bolts, cable ends, cables, turnbuckles, connections, lock pins, sail material, stitching, tubing, makeup of the airframe, harness design and other glider components. HMA also is insisting upon routine care, maintenance and inspection. Before earning HMA certification, glider types must be demonstrated for safety, stability and maneuverability.

Much hardware now comes direct from the aircraft industry. Helmets, improved harnesses, quick-release suspension devices, leading edges stiffened by cables, sail refinements, increased use of tough gloves and protective shoes, airspeed indicators, altimeters, and stall-warning sys-

131

*Saddleback Mountain with a 4,200-foot
drop is highest launching level
at Escape County outdoor recreational park.*

tems are realities which may increase safety. Scientists of the caliber of Lockheed's Irv Culver have contributed to the engineering literature of hang gliding. And for the first time in the history of human flight, scientific papers are being published on the little-understood, small-scale turbulence and air flows near the ground, which are affected by the terrain. (See "Micrometeorology and Hang Gliding" by Paul MacCready, Jr., *Ground Skimmer*, January, 1975.)

Some thinking is far-out: air bags to pop open in an instant to surround a crashing pilot; parachutes to deploy from kingposts; computerized robots for flight-testing new wings; forward-mounted energy absorbers — the latter an idea not so new, for as Otto Lilienthal noted: "I was saved from further hurt by the structure forward of my body." An oft-heard complaint — sometimes as an explanation for an accident — is that a hang glider pilot aloft, particularly flying prone, sees well only forward and down. Although it has never happened, the mid-air collision of craft composed of entangling wires and tubes and harnesses is a nightmare haunting all flyers. Tom Peghiny's idea of stitching windows of transparent material into the wings may help sort out the patterns at soaring sites.

Intentions of pilots can be critically im-portant where more than one kite is flying. Turning signal lights aid automotive traffic. Perhaps miniaturized versions on wingtips might enhance safety at little expense of money and weight.

Throughout the movement awareness grows that the best-made kite can become a turkey if it is out of trim. Landing and flying wires may loosen. A nose-in landing may induce a set in the keel boom. Small changes in the center of gravity drastically alter performance of some Rogallos. The word is spreading also that preventive maintenance is as crucial to hang gliding as it is in other forms of flight. One manufacturer, Ted Schmiedeke, calls on seven years as a project engineer with a major airline to advise his fellow pilots to be on the alert for corrosion. His terse program for avoiding structural fatigue appeared in the Fall, 1974, edition of *Hang Glider* magazine.

Analysts have concluded that the level of pilot involvement has progressed far beyond the level of pilot knowledge, and that this factor explains most accidents. The answer is one that has served humankind in so many ways from the beginning: education. Leaders such as Gerald Albiston recommend from experience that training schedules be extended, that progress in training should be gradual, that beginners should not fly winds greater than 12 mph,

132

that six months of steady flying should
precede attempts at 360-degree turns, and
that stunts (climbing into control bar,
hanging upside down from seat) should be
forbidden.

Flight schools — good ones — are considered as logical for hang gliding beginners as for novice airplane pilots. As one
teacher of 400 students wrote, "The hang
glider is an aircraft, and it should be approached accordingly. Selling an aircraft of
this type without instruction is like send-
ing a person on a solo flight in a Cessna for
his first encounter with the plane. Without
ground school or instruction-supervised
flight training, the pilot's odds of survival
are debatable." The United States Hang
Gliding Association today administers a
Hang Rating program which provides a
systematic rating of pilot skills. The prom-
ise is for a day when pilots of insufficient
ability will be dissuaded from going aloft at
sites and in conditions potentially beyond
their achievement.

The Accident Review Board of the Association currently is directed by Robert V.
Wills, whose interest poignantly is sharp-
ened by the loss of a son to the sport. A

summary of the findings of the first official meeting of the board suggested that most accidents involve trainees and novices in awkward, lowspeed crashes. But crashes with serious injury and fatality seem to overtake more intermediate or expert pilots who were "either trying the wrong maneuver at the wrong place or who ran into some unexpected wind conditions." Downwind landing was another cause identified as a major accident cause. Of the death of Eric, 20, the elder Wills told the *Los Angeles Times:* "He didn't know enough about kite flying. Even though it looks easy, it can be dangerous for anyone who pushes ahead too fast. We are convinced

the sport is here to stay. The problem is to educate the fliers, impress upon them the dangers, convince them the experts didn't learn overnight and persuade them never to risk injury by exceeding their capability."

Conflict with other outdoor users — even other fliers — is not unreconcilable. A world-famous soaring port existed at Torrey Pines long before Rogallos drifted over the horizon. After much discussion, practical experience and compromise, Torrey currently is used on busy days by hang gliders, sailplanes and radio-controlled model gliders. San Diego hang glider officials control landings and launches. Unacquainted pilots who cannot convince the regular users of Torrey Pines that they have the keen flying edge required for cliff soaring are emphatically informed to keep their kites folded up.

For certain, the sport either effectively will regulate itself, or receive increased attention from local, state and federal governments. Since May 16, 1974, hang gliding has been put on notice by the Federal Aviation Administration (Advisory Circular No. 60-10) that manufacturers and pilots bear responsibility of the future of the sport. Guidelines for operations are:

1. Limit altitude to 500 feet above the general terrain. It must be remembered, however, that there are certain aircraft operations conducted below 500 feet above the terrain and hang glider operators should be alert to this.

2. Do not fly them within controlled airspace, specifically a control zone, airport traffic area, or within five miles of the

boundary of an uncontrolled airport unless authorized by airport authorities.

3. Do not fly them within any prohibited or restricted area without prior permission from the controlling or using agency, as appropriate.

4. Do not fly them within 100 feet horizontally of, or at any altitude over, buildings, populated places, or assemblages of persons.

5. Remain clear of clouds.

6. Questions regarding operations in conflict with the above recommended safety parameters should be discussed with the nearest FAA district office.

If Guideline No. 1 were a law, the jails would be filled with hang glider pilots. Five hundred feet these days is considered a low altitude by many advanced pilots.

Some observers draw a parallel between hang gliding and scuba diving. When aqualung gear became available to great

numbers of people some twenty years ago, alarming numbers of free, air-breathing humans descended into another hostile realm. Inexperience, faulty equipment and unexpected dangers took an alarming toll of fishlike people.

By contrast, Scripps Institution of Oceanography approached scuba diving with careful, scientific methodology. It has the oldest, continuous scuba training program in the United States, and Scripps likely has taught more people the techniques of safe diving than any other school. Scripps oceanographers by now have dived in all the world's seas including the Arctic and Antarctic.

"Ours is a perfect safety record," says Jimmy Stewart, Scripps diving officer. "Our people have made 60,000 dives without accident. It has been a matter of pride, training, equipment and attitude."

Attitude may prove to be hang gliding's Achilles' heel. Memories are fresh of rogue pilots hanging upside down in their swing seats to interrupt the 1973 Nationals. When very low clouds invaded the F. M. Rogallo Hang Glider and Birthday Party, efforts of Meet Director Kas de Lisse to halt all flying were ignored. Hot dog flying, stunting and daredevil trips are still a part of the scene. California entrants in the National Soaring Festival in Frankfort, Michi-

137

gan, 1974, set a bad example by throwing off their helmets in mid-air.

Such behavior evoked a letter from Bob Skinner, Rogallo veteran:

Let's clean up our act. To fly is one of the most pleasurable experiences an individual could possibly have. It blends the beauty and forces of nature with the realm of true flight. For thousands of years people have wanted the opportunity to experience what some of us are experiencing now. There is a chapter in a book called The Third Eye *about having a master kite builder in a Tibetan Monk village long ago. The monks would climb inside a boxlike kite and be tethered up by the forces of wind funneling up through a ravine to great altitude. . . . one villager flew off in a wing-type kite and disappeared out of sight, never to be heard from again. They were really trying to do what we have the ability to do today.*

Unfortunately . . . those super egos that don't give a damn about anything but themselves, the ones that won't adhere to basic rules, as easy as they may be, are detrimental to the promising future of the miracle we have. . . .

Don't you think we are moving too fast? Maybe we're really missing what this gift was meant to be. Isn't it likely that through our own ignorance we're killing the reality of true flight? Why don't we slow down? Why don't we put on a helmet at flying sites that require one worn? Why don't we try to get along with those people who are into other ways of flying? Why don't we grow up?

There are some excellent fliers who are setting bad examples for the whole flying community. They may be super fliers, but they're missing the point somehow. Their indestructible attitude and the false illusions that anyone can easily learn to fly have to cease. Kite flying is a life-and-death situation.

The sentiment is echoed by he who made the wing.

We all deplore the deaths and injuries," Frances Rogallo *wrote to* Hang Glider

Caught in a moment of indecision,
a Rogallo pilot symbolizes the questions concerning
the future new–old sport of hang gliding.

Weekly. *"And I never suggest that hang gliding is not dangerous, but it can be a healthy and rewarding sport. I've made over 200 flights (and climbs back up the hill) this past year, and hang gliding has improved my physical health and condition.*

I would like to see the effort directed toward making hang gliding safer rather than more restricted or even prohibited. The development or improvement of aircraft and the determination of their characteristics is the application of science and engineering. Structural and aerodynamic faults of the gliders can be determined and eliminated by known scientific and engineering methods. There will always be some accidents resulting from lack of pilot skill or judgment, but perhaps these can be reduced through a vigorous educational effort.

The glory age of hang gliding may be when throughout the movement the *safest* pilot is hailed as the *best* pilot.

Acknowledgments

The creators of this book gratefully tip a wing in salute to two of organized hang gliding's earliest leaders, Lloyd Licher and Joe Faust, both of whom opened doors of research and provided encouragement. Although sportsmen of other loyalties, Publisher Paul Weaver and Editor Jim Howard quickly perceived the kinship of hang gliding with the twentieth century's other newly established pastimes: surfing, skiing, skindiving. Unless otherwise noted here, all photographs in this book are by Stephen McCarroll. Photos by Don Dedera appear on pages 22, 42, 43, 60, 68, 69, 71 (lower left), 78, 79, 82, 83, 85, 89, 92 (right), 102, 103, 105 (lower left), 109 (upper left), 114 (upper right), 116, 118, 120 and 121. Thanks are extended to the vintners of Annie Green Springs wine who provided the photography on pages 72 and 73, and to Sea World aquatic park for use of the aerial view on page 48. A special gesture of gratitude is offered to the editors of *Gallery* magazine who so generously granted permission to reprint a portion of the adventure which begins on page 8. The narrative originally appeared in *Gallery's* June, 1974 issue under the byline of Rich Taylor.

HANG GLIDING: *The Flyingest Flying*
WAS DESIGNED BY ROBERT JACOBSON
AND SET IN LINOTYPE ALDUS WITH VIVALDI DISPLAY.
IT WAS PRINTED ON MOHAVE MATTE PAPER
AND BOUND AT ROSWELL BOOKBINDING.